CW01645815

SNAPREVISE

SnapRevise Text Guide:
Twelfth Night
by William Shakespeare

Chelsea Rabl

InStudent Education UK Ltd owner of SnapRevise® trademark.
43 Priston Close, Worle, BS22 7FL, Weston-Super-Mare, United Kingdom

www.snaprevise.co.uk

Title: Twelfth Night by William Shakespeare Text Guide
ISBN: 978-1-917424-50-9

Published by InStudent Education UK Ltd CN 15550989 under licence from InStudent Publishing Pty Ltd.
ACN 624 188101

Preface

Hello! My name is Chelsea, and I'm a lover of reading, writing, acting, and Doctor Who. I graduated high school in 2018. Whether you're a student that's stressing, determined, or just a lover of the Bard, I look forward to our travels together into this delightful play.

"Delightful?" You say. Oh yes, dear reader, I hear your incredulity. Shakespeare tends to have a rather unfortunate reputation as stuffy, confusing, and a bit weird ("I did impeticos thy gratillity"... um, what? Those definitely aren't real words). But I hope you have the chance to see it performed over the course of your study, because Shakespeare still has the ability to be funny, heart-wrenching, and all the stuff that good theatre should be today. Personally, I was lucky enough to see three versions in 2018: a live outdoor performance by Shakespeare in the Park with onstage fire, audience sing-alongs, and dancing; the Melbourne Theatre Company's production with sets that fell from the ceiling and enchanting music played by skilled musicians dressed like fantasy elves; and the film adaptation directed by Trevor Nunn that I encourage you to watch for yourself. And no, you can't *just* watch the movie (although Helena Bonham Carter, Ben Kingsley, Imelda Staunton, and the whole cast are phenomenal). But if reading the play itself still seems daunting, never fear, that's what I'm here for! Equally, if you can't wait to dig in to some deeper analysis and consider different concepts, read on...

Come, let's explore Illyria together.

— Chelsea Rabl

Contents

Section 1

Nutshell Summary

Count Orsino is **infatuated** with the Countess Olivia, who refuses his **suit**.

Viola is washed ashore after a shipwreck, her twin brother presumed drowned. She disguises herself as a man in order to serve in Orsino's court. As 'Cesario', Viola quickly gains favour and is sent by Orsino to woo Olivia on his behalf. Viola does so reluctantly, having fallen in love with Orsino herself.

Olivia then falls in love with 'Cesario', forming a classic love triangle.

Viola's twin brother, Sebastian, is alive! A Captain called Antonio rescued him from the shipwreck. Sebastion looks exactly like his sister, who he assumes has drowned. Antonio cannot walk openly as he is a wanted man, so they arrange to meet up later.

Olivia's uncle Sir Toby Belch and the incompetent knight Sir Andrew **Ague**, a suitor to Olivia, spend their days in drunken rowdiness at her court, sometimes joined by Olivia's gentlewoman Maria, to the disdain of the steward Malvolio. He rebukes all three for some late-night revelry. In revenge, Maria forges a letter which convinces Malvolio that Olivia loves him, and that he should carry out various ridiculous actions if he loves her in return.

Viola/Cesario is sent again to Olivia, where the Countess confesses her love. Upset that Olivia shows more favour to Cesario than to himself, Sir Andrew challenges Viola/Cesario to a duel. Antonio, mistaking Viola for her brother, steps in to fight on 'Sebastian's' behalf. As he is dragged away by police, Antonio is upset that Viola does not recognise him. Viola begins to suspect that her brother is alive and leaves. Spurred on by Sir Toby, Sir Andrew follows to continue the fight.

Malvolio approaches Olivia, enacting the absurd instructions of Maria's forged love-letter. Olivia assumes he has gone mad and leaves him with Maria and Sir Toby, who delight in pretending he is possessed by Satan, and lock him up.

Sir Andrew fights Sebastian, believing him to be Cesario, and Olivia rushes to intervene. She begs forgiveness from Sebastian, also taking him for Cesario, who is at once confused and delighted by her tenderness, and agrees to marry her.

Infatuated: obsessed with passion for someone or something.

Suit: in this context, refers to the attempt to win a woman favour with a view to marriage.

Ague: a feverish illness such as malaria.

Finally, Orsino decides to visit Olivia himself, with Cesario/Viola tagging along. When Olivia rejects him again Orsino threatens to kill Cesario, despite his own strong affections for the page, suspecting her to be in love with 'him'. Dismayed at Viola/Cesario's willingness to die for the Count, Olivia reveals that they are married, to Viola's bafflement.

Sebastian enters. Everyone is amazed to see the identical Viola and Sebastion together, and they are overjoyed to have found one another. Orsino realises that Viola loves him, and agrees to marry her.

Malvolio arrives with the letter, which Olivia reveals was written by Maria (now married to Sir Toby), and he vows to be revenged.

The play is riddled with appearances from the fool Feste, who ends the play with a song about growing through life's stages, the chaos of human experience, and the hope that the audience enjoyed the play.

Section 2

Background Information

The author

William Shakespeare was born in 1564 in Stratford-upon-Avon, England. He attended grammar school as a boy, married Anne Hathaway (no not that one, the other one) when he was 18, then left her and their three children around eight years later to seek his fortune as an actor and playwright in London. Over the next 26 years, Shakespeare penned at least 37 plays and 154 sonnets, became part owner of the Globe Theatre, and won the favour of both Queen Elizabeth I and King James I. He died in 1616 aged 52.

A lot of people forget that Shakespeare was writing mostly for the entertainment of the common people, so most of his works have loads of comedy and exciting sword fights, as well as the more high-brow poetry and exploration of human nature stuff we're used to writing essays about! The fact that his works are still studied and performed today evidence just how brilliant this guy was at combining the two.

Seven years after his death, two of Shakespeare's fellow actors collated his works into what is known as the **First Folio**. Eighteen of the plays published therein had never before been printed, including *Twelfth Night*. If not for Shakespeare's mates, these works could well have been lost forever, and you wouldn't be studying this now (for better, or for worse). It was also in this Folio, only after the Bard's death, that Shakespeare's works were categorised for the first time according to their specific tropes and conventions into **tragedies, comedies, and histories**, groupings that we still use today.

KEY POINT :

Apart from his works, Shakespeare left behind no diary or means for us today to understand the way that he thought or what – if anything – he was trying to express through his plays. Therefore it is very important to never say 'Shakespeare thought...' or 'Shakespeare believed..." in your essays, **always refer to what the author implies or demonstrates *through the text* as opposed to their own opinions.** For example, just because 'The Taming of the Shrew' portrays a woman being tortured with sleep deprivation and starvation by her husband, *doesn't mean* that Shakespeare condoned this or was himself sexist.

The era

Shakespeare wrote during the **late sixteenth and early seventeenth centuries.** *Twelfth Night* was written around the turn of the century, while Queen Elizabeth I was still on the throne. There are a few points to keep in mind about life during the Elizabethan era when analysing *Twelfth Night,* as we'll examine now.

Life for women

When Viola decides to disguise herself as a man, it's not just a silly whim. Although she comes from a wealthy family – possessed of "gold", and of "soft and tender breeding" – she is washed ashore with nothing, so may as well be a commoner. In Elizabethan England, common women had no prospects of any formal education and were expected to get married, keep house and have children. But without a dowry it would be difficult to find a husband, so as a single woman Viola would have been compelled into a life of domestic servitude like Maria. This would totally *suck,* after a childhood filled with learning "many sorts of music", foreign languages (Sir Andrew: "Dieu vous garde, monsieur." Viola: "Et vous aussi; votre serviteur." – Act 3 Scene 1), and generally being spoiled with nice things. Disguised as a man, she is under no pressure to marry, commands greater respect, can earn a living as a minstrel or page, and need not fear any unwanted advances from men with wandering eyes or hands.

Critical perspectives: a literary term for 'lenses' through which you can choose to read and analyse a text, looking at how a particular feature is represented; (e.g. is the text biased? Is it realistic? Is it progressive or conservative?) Common critical perspectives include Feminism, Eco-criticism, Marxism, Queer Theory, Neo-Colonialism, and Psycho-analysis.

Life for gay men

Some modern interpretations of *Twelfth Night* take Antonio's self-proclaimed "love" for Sebastion to be homosexual rather than platonic. Likewise, Orsino is often played to have an attraction to Viola long before he is aware of her womanhood. These readings can lend depth to analysis of the play from a queer **critical perspective**, though what is explicit in the text is that Viola hides her own feelings towards Orsino due to her masculine disguise. Why is that? Because during the sixteenth centuary, homosexual relations were seen as both **criminal** and **sinful.** One prominent English academic at the time, John Rainold, described man-on-man sex as a "monstrous sin against nature." Obviously that's an awful thing to say – people have every right to love who they love regardless of gender. Nevertheless, the Elizabethans were a little hung up on it, (although they didn't have the labels of 'homosexual' and 'heterosexual' that we have today) so if you choose to argue for the potential homoeroticism of *Twelfth Night,* be aware that it would have been in **contravention to societal norms.** But, that wouldn't be the only way Shakespeare was being provocative with this play...

Elizabethan dress code

During the renaissance, **sumptuary laws** restricted what clothes people could wear in an attempt to regulate social station, social role, and gender. It was illegal for women to wear men's clothes, for the working classes to dress as nobility, and vice versa. Despite all being working class men (women were not yet allowed to act in the theatre), actors had a special exemption from this law to allow them to play all sorts of characters. So in the original presentation of Viola's character, there was a non-noble man pretending to be a noble woman pretending to be a non-noble man. More than just adding to the themes of disguise, Viola's choice shows her rebellious spirit.

Sumptuary: relating to laws about what people can and can't buy with their own private money.

Elizabethan theatre

Most of Shakespeare's work was performed at the Globe Theatre in London. This theatre was open to the sky, and rich people could come and pay for a seat with a cushion or a more expensive 'Lord's Room', but many of the audience were '**groundlings'** – people who only paid a penny to stand in the yard around the stage. People sometimes forget that much of Shakespeare's audience were common folk! So, far from being pretentious, many of his plays are full of rude jokes, ridiculous fights, and sexual innuendo (*Twelfth Night* included).

Theology: the study of God and religious beliefs.

The play

Shakespeare wrote *Twelfth Night* in the middle of his career. It was not the first time he had experimented with themes of mistaken identity, having written *Comedy of Errors* about seven years before, which also begins with twins being separated in a shipwreck. However, it is his only play with a double title; '***Twelfth Night'* or '*What You Will.'*** The first title refers to the festival on the Twelfth Night after Christmas – in Christian **theology**, this night marks the **Feast of the Epiphany,** celebrating the three wise men who brought gifts to baby Jesus. But for the Elizabethans, it marked the end of Yuletide revelry when they had the *biggest, craziest, drunkest party of the year*. Borrowing from the Roman tradition of **Saturnalia**, on Twelfth Night the Elizabethans would **turn social order upside-down.** A '**Lord of Misrule'** was often appointed to preside over the chaos, where servants were served by their masters, guests insulted, crazy clothes worn, everyone ate and drank and danced and all the normal rules were inverted for a day. This explains the many social transgressions and overall "madness" throughout the play, with Sir Toby as an ideal candidates for the 'Lord of Misrule' figure. Remember, though, that after the Twelfth Night festival, everything went back to normal, just as at the end of the play the characters are married off and the loose ends resolved. Consider then, that any comment Shakespeare *seems* to be making during the play's major action, of female empowerment, the **proletariat's** superiority, or the transcendence of love, is in fact the *opposite* of what society truly valued. The temporarily allowed misrule can be interpreted as an **orchestrated outlet for the oppressed** in order to prevent revolution, ultimately perpetuating oppression.

Saturnalia: the ancient Roman pagan festival over the winter solstice in mid-December honouring the agricultural god Saturn, from which many of our modern day 'Christmas' traditions are derived.

Proletariat: a term for the working class used most often in analyses from a Marxist critical perspective.

As for the second title, 'What You Will' could have many meanings. Indeed, **the deliberate double title reflects the multiple possible meanings of the text,** both in the many double meanings in the dialogue, and the **macrocosmic** interpretations of the play. Here is a list of some other possible interpretations of "What You Will" as a title. They are not necessarily mutually exclusive, more than one could be right! You are of course welcome to come up with your own ideas as well. In English, **there is no single 'right' answer. Anything you can provide a credible and evidenced argument for is valid.**

Macrocosm: the whole complex structure of the world or universe, as opposed to a small representative part (microcosm). From Latin, meaning big (macro) universe/world (cosmos).

- 'Will' could refer to desire, as much of the play is about **forbidden love.**
- 'What You Will' invites us, the audience, to make of the play 'what [we] will' (i.e. interpret it as we see fit).
- 'What You Will' reflects the characters' **hedonism.**
- Shakespeare was having a bit of a laugh and though he'd put his own name in the title. (William. Get it? What You *Will*. Haha... yeah, don't put that in your essay.)

Another important piece of context is that *Twelfth Night* is a **comedy.** In Shakespearean terms, **the key distinction between a comedy and tragedy is the outcome for the protagonist** In most, although not all, of the plays listed in the First Folio as 'Comedies,' the protagonist achieves their goal and ends in a state of happiness, and most of the plot's loose ends are tied up in a neat little bow. In general terms, everything is good, then chaotic, then great. Here, most of the characters end up married in a happily-ever-after, let's-all-have-a-good-laugh-and-ride-off-into-the-sunset scenario. (By contrast, in tragedies, the protagonist often has a fatal flaw that leads to their downfall, and many characters often end up dead. Cheery, right?)

Hedonism: the pursuit of pleasure or self-indulgence throughout the play.

Protagonist: the main character(s).

Finally, let's talk about Shakespearean conventions common to all of his plays. **Shakespeare used very few stage directions** in his work, except where completely unavoidable, so all of the jokes, physical comedy, and the relationships between the characters must be figured out from clues in the dialogue. **It's a good idea to pay attention to imagery,** as this is used to set the tone for most scenes. For example, Orsino's opening monologue establishes many of the themes that Shakespeare returns to throughout the play (more detail on that in the next section) and sets a tone of **melancholy**.

Melancholy: a feeling of passive, thoughtful sadness.

Shakespeare also does something clever with the structure of dialogue; often, you can tell how educated a character is by whether they speak in **verse or prose**. Generally, upper classes speak in verse, and lower classes in prose. However, if a member of the upper classes is drunk, stupid, or speaking with less pretension, they are more likely to speak in prose, like Sir Toby and Sir Andrew. Likewise, when moved to great emotion, a member of the lower classes may speak in verse, such as when Antonio believes Sebastian has betrayed him in Act 3 Scene 4: *"In nature there's no blemish but the mind: / None can be called deformed but the unkind."*

Two more features typical to Shakespeare are the **soliloquy** and **dramatic irony.** A soliloquy is a **monologue** where a character speaks their thoughts out loud to the audience, but no other characters on stage can hear them – for example, the famous, "to be or not to be" speech from *Hamlet*. Dramatic irony is when we (the audience) know something that the characters don't (e.g. we know that 'Cesario' is a woman, while Olivia believes she is falling in love with a man).

Alright then. On with the show!

Verse: this is another word for poetry. Sometimes verse will rhyme, but not always. You can tell a passage is verse by its format (broken lines grouped into stanzas) or its rhythm when spoken aloud.

Prose: writing in its normal form, without structured rhyme or metric rhythm. You can think of prose as being like paragraphs.

/: the forward slash is used when quoting verse to indicate that we have moved on to the next line.

Section 3

Scene-by-Scene Analysis

Act 1 Scene 1

The Duke Orsino listens to music while languishing for the love of Olivia with his servants. The Duke's wealth and high status are evident from his **exclusive use of verse, the fact that the entire first scene is dedicated to him, and his elevated language.** However, the connotations of the images he crafts suggest that **Orsino isn't actually in love with Olivia; rather, he is in love with the idea of love itself.**

Temperamental: behaving erratically or having sudden mood swings.

Orsino is clearly **temperamental,** moving in one line from lengthy praise of a "strain" of music, to suddenly declaring "no more. / 'Tis not so sweet now as it was before." Similarly, he compares love to the ocean, in that "Nought enters" love that within "a minute" is not worthless, thus implying that should he achieve Olivia's love he would no longer want it. Indeed, he states explicitly **"that [love] alone is high fantastical."**

Furthermore, his only description of Olivia is that "her sweet perfections" "purged the air of pestilence." By contrast, he describes himself as having "noblest eyes," being like "a hart" pursued by his "desires... cruel hounds," a "selfsame king." When Orsino is informed that Ollvia intends to wear a veil and cry every day for seven years in mourning of her brother, he doesn't empathise with her grieving like someone who really cared might; instead, he looks forward to one day dominating Olivia above "all affections else." **He talks about himself more frequently and with more specific praise than the woman he professes to love and shows no empathy for her loss, suggesting a preoccupation with narcissistic melancholy rather than true affection.**

Abatement: ending or subsiding. In this case, the word means death.

Brine: salty water

In his opening monologue, Orsino's range of reference is vast; from "music" to "appetite" to a "bank of violets." By using imagery to paint pictures in the audience's mind, the characters can add to the fantastical nature of the play, and the blending of all these particular images together addresses multiple human senses (hearing, taste, sight, smell) in order to **make love appear all-encompassing.**

The imagery of this scene also **foreshadows** the next one. Here, love is described "as the sea," which has the "capacity" to take everything and make it "fall into **abatement**." Another reference to the ocean is the description of Olivia's tears for her dead brother as "eye-offending **brine**." In the next scene, as we will see, Viola also cries for her brother, who has been taken by the sea and assumed to "fall into abatement." She herself also entered the waves of "validity and pitch" as a wealthy woman, and as she leaves "falls into... low price," disguising herself as a commoner.

Act 1 Scene 2

Viola is washed ashore with a Captain who saved her following a shipwreck in which she believes her brother has drowned. The Captain comforts her with the suggestion that maybe he survived. He also informs her about the state of affairs in Illyria, including Orsino's suit and Olivia's vow, and Viola decides to disguise herself as a **eunuch** to serve Orsino.

Like Orsino, we see that Viola (and the Captain) have an education and relatively high status as they speak in **verse.** We also know that **Viola is rich** because she offers the Captain "gold," and that she is noble by association with Orsino, who her "father name[d as a] bachelor" some years before. The gap between the classes is set out here, suggesting that the bourgeoisie are "great ones" and the proletariat "less[er]." This **classism** is also reflected in the play's structure; The first two scenes are given to people with power and wealth. **Illyria is thus a country with a strong class structure** based on wealth and familial nobility. But **the mere existence of classism is not necessarily an endorsement** of it, indeed this **set of social rules is immediately blurred** or broken by Viola's decision to "disguise" herself as a common servant.

This scene follows a similar structure to the former, both relating a great deal of **exposition** within a few pages, and an emotional arc that transitions from intense emotion into swift action. **The juxtaposition of Viola's grief and Orsino's 'love' in consecutive scenes presents a microcosm to the extremities of emotion that will be present in the play.**

There are two more important points in this scene.

Firstly, we have the Captain's allusion to "Arion." According to Greek mythology, Arion leapt into the sea to escape pirates, then climbed onto a dolphin's back and began to play his lyre. This allusion thus marks another image in which **music (the lyre), the ocean, and love (Viola's brother), are intertwined** (the other being Orsino's metaphors in Scene 1). The repetition of these connections encourages us to associate the various attributes of music and the ocean, and apply them to love. For instance, love can be as enchanting as a melody, yet as dangerous as crashing waves. And unreciprocated love drives us as wild as the ocean, but when our beloved plays its song back to us, like Arion, the waves are calmed. **Remember, there is no single right answer. With imagery, pick the analysis that makes the most sense and supports your discussion of the play as a whole.**

Secondly, Viola's repetition of "perchance" is an early iteration of a specific character trait of hers – namely throwing her hands in the air and practically saying *'whatever'*. It happens again at the end of the scene, and she says "what else may hap, to time I will commit". In other words: *'I dunno, whatever's gonna happen is time's problem, not mine.'*

Eunuch: a castrated man. Eunuchs were often employed as musicians as they could sing higher than the average man.

Classism: prejudice against people of a lower social status, and privilege for those of higher.

Exposition: explanation of background information to the world and plot; the who, what, when, where, why, and how of the story.

Juxtaposition: when two opposing images or ideas are placed together to create contrast.

Microcosm: a small part representative of the whole.

Archetype: a typical example of an abstract idea.

This passivity allows her to maintain the archetype of the damsel in distress despite her active involvement in the plot: although she runs around doing stuff, her disguise allows her to distance herself from her actions and her refusal to accept responsibility means that she may as well be pining away in a tower like a princess in a fairy tale.

Act 1 Scene 3

Aptronym: a person's name that is amusingly reflective of their occupation or personality.

Caustic: in this context, a sarcastic and scathing joke.

Materialism: the belief that material possessions (money, a big house, beautiful clothes) are more important than things like spirituality, love, and happiness.

Patriarchy: a system of society in which men hold the power and women are largely excluded from it.

At Olivia's house, her gentlewoman Maria chastises a drunk Sir Toby Belch, Olivia's cousin, for coming in so late. He is followed by Sir Andrew Aguecheek, a hopeful suitor to Olivia whose idiocy is demonstrated in a match of wits with Maria. She leaves the men to continue their fun, and Sir Andrew's gullibility is again shown as Sir Toby convinces him to stay in Illyria (and keep funding Toby's drinking habit) despite Olivia's total lack of interest.

Finally, we get some prose! At last! But here we see how the manner of a **character's speech reflects not only their status, but also their state of mind.** Both Sir Toby and Sir Andrew are noblemen, as discernible by their titles alone, and Sir Toby's education is evident in his clever wordplay ("let her except, before excepted") and knowledge of Latin and French. This makes them perfect candidates for verse, save one thing; they are quite drunk. Also, Sir Andrew is an idiot. To further prove their comedic nature, Shakespeare employs **aptronyms**, naming Sir Toby *Belch* after the sound he makes after drinking too much, and Sir Andrew *Ague*cheek after malaria.

This 'bringing down' of the bourgeoisie to the level of the lower class Maria is another clear **breach of class structure and social norms.**

Further to this, despite her status as a mere servant, Maria is clearly one of the cleverest characters in the play (we shall see further instances of her ingenuity as we continue). Here, she makes a "dry jest" of Sir Andrew, besting her superior with a **caustic** remark. She also uses her femininity to make him uncomfortable; when she invites Sir Andrew to "bring [his] hand to th'buttery-bar" she is referring to her breast, and the "dry[ness]" of his hand is a double entendre referring to his inability to arouse a woman. **Thus Maria displays her sexual and intellectual empowerment despite being both a woman and worker, the embodiment of the oppressed.** Hence, we can say that Shakespeare is questioning the validity of **materialistic patriarchy,** and perhaps implying that it is somewhat obsolete.

This is a very funny scene, filled with verbal and physical comedy. Departing from the exposition, Shakespeare has a chance to just give the audience some fun here, with Sir Andrew often played as a truly terrible dancer. We also have another reference to **disguised identity** in Sir Andrew's declaration that he "delight[s] in masques and revels." Thus, the audience is likewise encouraged to "delight" in the misrule to come.

Act 1 Scene 4

Within three days of serving Count Orsino, Viola has become one of his favourite and most trusted servants. He asks her to present his suit to Olivia and not take no for an answer. Viola agrees, but admits in an **aside** that she herself loves Orsino.

The jump in time from Viola's arrival on the beach to three days into Orsino's service is one of only two explicit **quantifications** of Shakespeare's manipulation of passing time in Twelfth Night. The other is in the very final scene, allowing the action in between to occur with a sense of **timeless ambiguity.** This **atemporality** adds to the distancing of the action from socially mandated morality, the clock being yet another convention to which society adheres. Just as Sir Toby and Sir Andrew came in late in the last scene, the rest of the characters (and we, the audience) are permitted from this scene forward to largely **forget about the clock, and follow their socially transgressive whims.**

Another interesting note is Shakespeare's choice to make it *three* days later. This could totally have been a random number pulled from the air, but the next (and last) quantification of passed time (in the last scene) is also *three* months. Intentional or not, **the use of three evokes European folklore tradition** (Goldilocks and the Three Bears, The Three Little Pigs, Three Billy Goats Gruff... need I go on?), and as such adds to the fanciful tone of the play.

As for the characters and action itself, let's talk about the *chemistry* between Viola and Orsino. I mean hot *damn*. It's only been three days, and Orsino has already "unclasped / To [Viola] the book of [his] secret soul" and given her "favours" over all his other servants, while she has fallen so deeply in love that she wants to be his "wife"! **The pace and extremity of their emotions matches the tones and frantic pace of the past four scenes.** Thus, Shakespeare portrays a **gamut** of infatuation, grief, drunken cheer, and now love – none of which (when I read them aloud with a stopwatch) have exceeded four minutes of stage time.

Compare Orsino's vague praises of Olivia in the first scene to his attention to 'Cesario' here. There is a genuine affection and specificity in his praise of the "Dear lad", of their "youth" and "rubious" lip, that almost matches his original narcissism. Perhaps he does not yet know it, or discounts it as mere fondness, but it is clear that Orsino has a truer relationship with the person he calls Cesario that the wistful image he holds in his head of Olivia.

Aside: a remark to the audience that the other characters on stage don't hear – kind of like a really short soliloquy.

Quantification: the expression or measurement of the exact amount of something.

Atemporal: existing without relation to time.

Gamut: a wide range, scope, or spectrum.

Act 1 Scene 5

Enter Feste! The **fool** has been absent from Olivia's court for an unspecified period of time. He banters with Maria before Olivia arrives, at which point Olivia tells her servants to "Take the fool away", but Feste regains her favour by wittily riddling that *she* is the fool for mourning her brother's soul being in heaven. Her steward Malvolio is not so won over.

Fool: in this context, a professional jester; like a private comedian.

As discussed in the previous scene's analysis, the vague and unspecified nature of Feste's lateness reflects the transition of the play as a whole into atemporality. However **the fact that Feste himself is late and yet manages to win back favour so quickly demonstrates that he as an individual already exists outside of the rule of time.**

Feste, like Maria, also transcends the rules of class; despite their non-nobility they are both incredibly witty and knowledgeable, Feste knowing Latin ("cucullus non facet monachum," meaning 'the hood makes not the monk,' or, in other words, the clothes one wears does not determine one's identity), and Maria knowing the origin of the saying "I fear no colours". Feste is also incredibly perceptive, picking up on the flirtation between Maria and Sir Toby ("if Sir Toby would leave drinking, thou wert as witty a piece of Eve's flesh" (i.e. 'if Toby wasn't drunk all the time, you two would totally get together'), so the two are clearly friends.

Feigned: insincere or fake

When Olivia enters she makes a bold statement, not in what she says, but in how. She is the first noble of sound mind to speak in prose. Paired with her assertion later in this scene that "poetical" declarations are "more like to be **feigned**," it can be understood that **Olivia objects to pretension and ceremony.** This may reflect the fact that **as a woman with power in the patriarchy of Illyria, she is in the unique position to empathise with the oppression of the lower classes** despite her influence. Hence her speaking plain English to them without condescension, and her forgiveness of Feste. It is also logical that she would reject Orsino's suit – marriage would see him assume all of her wealth and influence, taking away her independence.

Malvolio's introduction is wonderfully representative of his character. **His clinical language reflects his very uptight nature** and, although neither his class nor emotion would permit a foray into verse, extreme pretentiousness. Quite in contrast to Olivia, he is a member of the working class with ambitions above his station and disdain for all who dare to buck the system. As she puts it, Malvolio is "sick of self-love."

Meta-textual: when the author of a text self-consciously alludes to the artificiality or literariness of the work.

An unidentified gentleman arrives at the gate wishing to speak with Olivia. Sir Toby (being drunk) cannot describe him. Malvolio (being literal-minded) describes him after prompting as a youth, somewhere between a boy and man. Olivia assumes the gentleman is another messenger from Orsino and agrees to hear him out. It's a bit cheeky of old Shakespeare really, to have Olivia tell Malvolio to do "what you will" to dismiss Orsino's suit. This is one of a few **meta-textual** jokes for the audience. The others are Viola's declarations that "I swear, I am not that I play" and that "I have studied, and that question's out of my part." Both are logical within the play's context – Viola is not a boy, and she cannot yet reveal that she comes on Orsino's behalf lest she be sent away. However, like Olivia's use of "what you will," both have more meaning from the audience's perspective; the actor playing Viola was not a woman (in Shakespeare's day), and, being an actor, cannot reveal what is "out of [their] part."

This dramatic irony and layering of meaning draws attention to the artifice of the play, reminding the audience that they are watching a performance, and **thus justifies the farcical reactions as entertainment rather than reality** – instead of allowing the ridiculousness of the action to distance the audience, the play parodies itself to unite the performers and the audience in the ridicule of the characters.

There is also some **foreshadowing** here with Feste's line "the fool shall look to the madman." In Act 4 Scene 2, Feste looks to Malvolio, who is made out to be mad. This line also **distinguishes between fools and madmen,** such as to support Feste's claim that despite the reputation of his profession he is very clever ("I wear not motley in my brain"). It also **affords Feste a kind of invulnerability to the chaos and love,** often referred to within the play as 'madness,' that is soon to follow.

Viola (disguised as Cesario) wins a private audience with Olivia in which the Countess lifts her mourning veil to show her face (as she had vowed *not* to do for seven years). Viola acknowledges Olivia's beauty but rebukes her for her pride, and offers poetic adorations on Orsino's behalf. Olivia dismisses this suit but grows increasingly interested in 'Cesario,' fantasising about him after Viola leaves. Olivia sends Malvolio after her with a ring she claims was left as an unwelcome gift from Orsino.

Interestingly, Olivia initially hides her identity as the lady of the house. Like Viola's disguise as 'Cesario,' this is another example of a noble hiding their nobility. You've got to ask why this is such a prevalent instinct. It could be taken as evidence that **the freedoms of the proletariat are envied by the bourgeoisie;** anonymity, and freedom from reputation for example. However you choose to interpret it, it certainly **challenges the notion of identity,** suggesting perhaps that it could be **performative rather than innate.**

Once her servants are gone, Olivia displays the full extent of her scathing wit. She interrupts and challenges Viola at every turn, **presenting a stark contrast to her dreamy hopefulness once Viola leaves, and thus a benchmark from which to measure the effects of her love of Cesario.**

But what kind of love is it? We have analysed Orsino's 'love' of Olivia to be self-indulgent melancholy, and his love of 'Cesario' to be trusting fondness. How could we describe Olivia's love for the disguised Viola? The aspects that she praises as "perfections" are "[His] tongue, [his] face, [his] limbs, actions, and spirit." In true Olivia style, these are not elaborated on poetically, rather mentioned plainly, evidencing her sincerity. What's more, they represent a cross section of his whole person; the first three are physical, however "actions" and "spirit" prevent this from being merely lust. While still in its early stages, **it seems Olivia's feelings for Cesario are a genuine love for him as a full person.**

However, her question about his parentage shows that she is also concerned with marrying someone of a lower class, probably so that she can maintain some of her status in the event of their marriage. Despite her aforementioned sympathy to the proletariat, **her sense of superiority is still evident in her attempts to buy Cesario's love with money and gifts,** the ring she sends with Malvolio being the first of many.

When describing love, **elemental imagery** is employed. Notice Viola's description of Orsino's "groans that thunder love... sighs of fire," and desiring within a hypothetical scenario that Olivia "should not rest / Between the elements of air and earth" for love of her in return, if she was in Orsino's position. This link between love and nature is consistent with the previous **allusions to the ocean,** and continuing imagery throughout the play. Therefore remember whenever you spot references to nature that Shakespeare is likely also drawing a **metaphor for human emotion** – in this case, its untameable passion.

Finally, Olivia makes an appeal to fate in the last line of the Act. This delegation to supernatural forces is similar to Viola's reliance on chance (of which we will see more in Viola's next scene), however Olivia's is a specific and actionable appeal (*pleasepleaseplease let Cesario fall in love with me*), whereas Viola's is a vague abandonment to fate's will (*eh, what will be, will be*). Nevertheless, the similarity betrays a sense of **fatalism.** This could again be meta-textual as characters in a play certainly *don't* have control over their lives. However it could also contribute to the sentiment of powerlessness invoked by emotion, **a depiction of the vulnerability exposed when we allow ourselves to love.**

Fatalism: believing that everything is predetermined and inevitable, and that we cannot do anything to change our fates.

Act 2 Scene 1

The new act opens with a revelation: Viola's brother is alive! He was saved from the shipwreck by sea captain Antonio. Having hidden his identity until now, Sebastian reveals his nobility and the presumed death of his sister. He decides to go to Orsino's court without Antonio for fear of sharing his bad luck. Antonio has enemies in Orsino's court, but follows him anyway.

This scene parallels Act 1 Scene 2 when Viola washed ashore, although this one lacks the extensive exposition that was necessary to the first. Once again, we see **the grief of a lost sibling,** and the wish to have shared in each others' fate; where Viola hoped that he survived, Sebastian wishes he had died with her in the waves. Once again, we see **the instinct to disguise** oneself; Sebastian told Antonio that his name was Roderigo so he would not be recognised as the son of his reputed father "Sebastion of Messaline." And once again, **the saviour** is a good person who is not disguised; Viola describes her captain's mind to match his "fair and outward character," while Sebastian recognises Antonio's "modesty" and "love." Obviously, this structural similarity reflects the respective subjects being literal twins.

Sebastian's survival also evolves the oceanic imagery; where before love, like the sea, was something wild which took as much as it gave. Now having returned Sebastian alive the ocean appears far more benevolent, and thus **it is suggested that love may also be kind**.

So, what kind of character is Sebastian himself? Like his sister he has a preoccupation with "fate," even a belief that his misfortune might be contagious. He is modest in his opinion of himself, managing to downplay his own appearance *and* call his sister beautiful... even though they look nearly identical.

KEY POINT :
Viola and Sebastian are not identical twins. Identical twins occur when one egg splits in the womb, and both babies share the same genetic code. That would mean they both have to be the same sex. These two are fraternal twins, which means there were two seperate original eggs, so they only share the same amount of genetics as normal siblings. The fact that they look so similar is just a coincidence, so just make sure you don't use the term 'identical twins' in your essay!

Sebastian is also quick in his praising of others, mentioning Olivia's beautiful brain. He clearly has an awareness of the prestige that his identity affords him, yet disguised himself initially, refuses Antonio's offer to be his servant, and like Olivia **chooses to speak in prose so as not to impose his status.** Basically, he's a really nice guy whose **behaviour suggests a sense of egalitarianism.**

Egalitarianism: the belief in equality between all people.

However, her also refers to open sadness as "the manners of [his] mother," and appears ashamed to cry even in front of a beloved friend. Sebastian also never explicitly says that he loves Antonio, although Antionio says a number of times that he "love[s]" and "adore[s]" him. Thus, **Sebastian subscribes to a definition of masculinity which is sees explicate emotion as weak and feminine.** On the other hand, **Antonio represents a vision of masculinity which freely expresses itself and is not threatened by declarations of love** or (more traditionally) physical danger either. Notice also how Antonio (unlike Orsino with Olivia) empathises with Sebastian's loss – his love and humanity is genuine.

Pay attention to how each of these characters fare throughout the play; **which version of manhood will be rewarded?**

Act 2 Scene 2

Malvolio gives Viola the ring that Olivia claimed she had left with her. He leaves and Viola has a fun little monologue, realising that Olivia is in love with her and freaking the hell out.

Viola's monologue is full of quotational gems, explicitly bringing together many of the themes of the play.

Firstly, she discusses the nature of **disguise and identity.** Viola distinguishes, not for the first time, between the outer and inner self. It *is* the first time, however, that she acknowledges the downfalls of "disguise... a wickedness," lamenting the confusion and limitations that it has caused and making no mention of its benefits to her (see page 4 for more on what life was like for women at the time).

Viola also makes contribution to the **feminist critical perspective** and any discussion concerning gender. In one single line she describes "women's" emotional "frailty" and shirks any responsibility for her predicament, blaming instead her feminine nature (as in, '*I can't help myself, I'm just a helpless woman.*')

Speaking of Viola's **submission to stereotypical helplessness,** we have another instance of **fatalistic** shifting of responsibility onto universal forces/entities; "O time, thou must untangle this, not I; / It is too hard a knot for me t'untie." Classic Viola. **Where other characters lose self-control in the face of love, Viola denies agency in the face of life.**

Act 2 Scene 3

After midnight, the ever-drunken Sir Toby and Sir Andrew have Feste to sing them a song. Feste asks whether they want "a love song, or a song of good life", implying that they can't have both. This is consistent with the melancholy that seeking love evokes in all characters, as summarised by Viola in the last scene. **The only character who may be said to live a truely "good life" is Feste, in love's absence** – Viola, Orsino, and Olivia pine for their loves, Malvolio and Sebastian will become convinced they are mad for theirs, Antonio will find himself imprisoned, Sir Andrew manipulated out of his money, and Sir Toby squalors in drink to disregard his status enough to be friendly with Maria, while she may love who she pleases because she is poor. Pick your poison; love, or good life?

Predictably, they choose love, and Feste sings the first song with lyrics in the play; **'O mistress mine.'** The first verse appeals to an unnamed woman to end her roaming journey and meet her love. This may **symbolise the freedom lost when women take a husband,** consistent with the **use of the possessive,** 'mine,' as opposed to 'my mistress,' denoting the woman as property of the **narrative voice** Here, Feste is not asking a woman to "trip no further" – that is the song's narrative voice. The second verse questions the nature of love and youth, concluding that **life and love are temporary**, and should be grasped in the moment. This call to "present laughter" reflects the greater play, as a comedy, and the reminder of decay reinforces the melancholy established from the very first scene as intertwined with love. They both then join Feste in singing a **catch**, in which Sir Andrew sets aside his title as knight, allowing himself to be called "knave" in the name of good fun, **once again breaching class structure conventions.** Maria warns them that they are too loud, and Malvolio arrives to really tell them off. He threatens Sir Toby that Olivia may banish him if he doesn't behave, and Sir Toby is very angry at being rebuked by a mere servant. Malvolio scolds Maria as well, and leaves.

Malvolio is right. The revellers have "no respect of place, persons, nor time," thus **enacting the epitome of Saturnalian misrule** (see page 5). **Ironically, in reprimanding his superiors for it, Malvolio actually adds to this contravention of societal norms.** It is Sir Toby who reminds him of his place as a lowly "steward." In this moment, Sir Toby embraces the previously rejected privilege of his station, and also of his gender in commanding Maria to fetch "a stoup of wine," and we see that he gladly abandons his egalitarian ideals when it suits him. Thus, **the classism and sexism of Illyria as shown to be deeply ingrained** in its people.

Narrative voice: the 'I' in a story. This sometimes differs from the narrator, who is the one telling the story.

Catch: in music refers to a round, often with funny lyrics and an easy upbeat tune

Epitome: the perfect example of something.

Maria, with Sir Toby's eager support, plans revenge; she will write a letter to make Malvolio believe Olivia is in love with him. Maria's intelligence finally comes into full view, as she uses elevated language and crafts a cunning plan, entirely contradicting her socially determined role to be quiet and yielding to men and her 'betters.' Sir Toby, reverting to his seemingly feminist behaviours, prefers to hear her plan rather than continue with his own (to stage a duel between Sir Andrew and Malvolio), and offers high praise in calling her "**Penthesilea**," while Malvolio is described as a "**puritan**." He also had good reason to, as puritans hated theatre and were renowned as highly strict individuals. (By 1648 they would be in charge of Parliament, and destroy the Globe Theatre!) The word is used as an insult, and **its negative connotations cast him as a symbol of strict adherence to the rules.** Thus, in plotting to "make him a common recreation," the trio are in fact taking **vengeance on the entire societal system** that sees them sidelined.

Penthesilea: Queen of the Amazons, and daughter of the Greek god of war, Ares.

Putrian: this was a religious group of English Protestants active during the Elizabethan era but without royal approval (meaning that Shakespeare was fairly safe in making fun of them!).

Act 2 Scene 4

Orsino and Viola chat about love, and Orsino calls for Feste to sing 'Come away death.' Viola challenges Orsino's declaration that women are less devoted than men, telling of her own predicament (forbidden love) under the guise of speaking about a fictional sister. Orsino sends her to woo Olivia again.

Orsino is still the highest status character of the play, and hence he persistently speaks in verse. So it's interesting that he **claims not to care about Olivia's wealth and "lands," but only for her beauty.** And although it's kind of nice that he's not taking advantage of her for her money, seeking her only for her physical attractiveness is still extremely shallow. The high value he places on physical beauty is further shown in his strong opinion that men must take women younger than themselves, as women's "fair flower / Being once displayed doth fall that very hour." **Being a common symbol for both beauty and virginity, this 'flower' simile thus betrays Orsino's sexism.**

And Viola agrees! This *could* be her just acting the part of the male 'Cesario,' but we can also interpret this as **evidence that the sexism of Illyria is so implicit as to have taught even the women that their worth is in their looks.** More boldly, it could be said to reflect Shakespeare's **bias as a male,** and the views of Elizabethan England.

Key Point :
While discussing ideas such as sexism, be careful not to apply modern standards too strictly. Despite not necessarily being in step with modern feminism (or many other civil rights or progressive movements for that matter), consider the impact the play would have had on its original audience and avoid going on any rants! Generally, academic essays should consider the subject in a **balanced and logical** way and consider what commentary the text is presenting, not whether it is morally wrong or right.

Orsino's other main traits, **temperamentality** and high opinion of himself, are also reinforced in this scene. He generalises his own traits of being "unstaid and skittish" to all lovers, and of being "giddy and unfirm" to all men, simultaneously admitting to his inconsistencies and demonstrating his **narcissistic tendency to view himself as the epitome of both romance and manliness.** He also contradicts himself, initially saying that that women are more constant than men "however we do praise ourselves," then claiming that "no woman [could have] so strong a passion" as men have. Feste notes that Orsino's "mind is a very opal," opal being a stone renowned for the changeability of its colours under the light, thus a metaphor illustrating the fickle nature of Orsino's emotions.

Feste is also perceptive of **Orsino's propensity for self-indulgent melancholy.** The song that he is asked to sing, 'Come away death,' is a melting pot of love and music and despondence. Like the fool's previous song, it **highlights the transience of love and life.**

Let's talk imagery. Orsino's talking about love, so we should expect by now to see a few things: comparisons to food, music, the ocean. Oh, what's that Orsino? Your love "is all hungry as the sea," and music "relieve[s your] passion... More than light airs?" Yeah. I thought so. At this point, there's not much I can say about these images that I haven't already said. **The consistency of this imagery shows us that Orsino's understanding of love has not evolved,** and that **the play is still in a state of chaos and sensory overload.** However from this point forward, we start to see a new image take over, specifically one of the garden. Here, in a moment of intense dramatic irony, Viola defends the passion of women by describing her "concealment [as] like a worm i'th'bud," depicting an inchworm destroying a budding rose. I'll point out more examples as **garden Images arise with more and more frequency, while the image of the hungry sea abates in inverse proportion.** Unlike the ocean, the Elizabethan garden is orderly, strictly planned and pruned, and follows the rule of the seasons. Thus **in the rise of garden imagery, the decline of madness and misrule will be reflected.**

Finally, just note that Orsino sends a "jewel" to Olivia via Viola, just as Olivia sent a ring to Viola via Malvolio. Each, from their position of superiority over their crush, seek to buy love, and each find, rather against capitalist wisdom, that love cannot be bought.

Act 2 Scene 5

Sir Toby, Sir Andrew, and Olivia's servant Fabian, a new character, hide to watch Malvolio's reaction to Maria's letter. He arrives, already fantasising about being a Count and married to Olivia, when he sees it on the ground. Reading out loud, he becomes convinced that it is a love letter from Olivia to him, despite no signing of the author nor naming of the letter's subject. He hurries to comply with the letter's instructions, to spurn Sir Toby, smile, and wear yellow cross-gartered stockings (an utterly ridiculous fashion). Maria hurries the three, all dying of laughter, towards Olivia to watch for Malvolio's transformation.

Fabian is the lowest status individual in the play. Although there are other low-profile servants, such as Orsino's Curio and Valentine (I forgive you if you don't remember who they are), Fabian's position in Olivia's household is clearly lower as he does not wait on his master directly, indeed does not even speak with her until the very end of the play, and even then only in rather **extenuating** circumstances. Along with Feste, Fabian is also one of only two characters (excepting Orsino's aforementioned servants, whose measly total of seven lines of pure exposition make them fairly insignificant) whose judgement is not confused by love. Thus, as an objective witness and enabler of the chaos reaped by Sir Toby and the gang, **Fabian is a reflection of the audience.**

Exteneuating: something that makes one's actions more forgivable.

Malvolio, in this case, is the performance. However **Malvolio's behaviour in this scene, as he believes himself to be alone, is the truest representation of his character** that there is. And basically, that character is a power hungry narcissist. The ease with which he believes the implausible idea of Olivia's love for him and accepts without question the letter's bizarre instructions betray both his inordinately high opinion of himself and desperation for the power fantasy in which he indulges. Like Orsino, **he wishes to be married to Olivia but shows no love for her.** In his entire monologue preceding the letter, he only mentions her once. The rest is about his imagined wealth and power over her estate, his hypothetical influence over Sir Toby. There is also the worrying connotations of his attempt "to crush this a little, [and force it to] bow to me," suggesting a tendency to seek domination over others.

Contrast this to Sir Toby's relationship with Maria. In this scene again are many examples of his specific and creative compliments of her character and wit (as opposed to simply appearance) affectionately calling her a "most excellent devil of wit" and "metal of India," describing *her* as gold rather than to care for her worldly affects (how very Marxist). Furthermore, **where Orsino seeks to rule Olivia as a "king" and Malvolio wishes only to become a "Count", Sir Toby offers himself as Maria's "bondslave." Thus Sir Toby's love is once again proven the most genuine, and his character the most feminist**.

As for Maria's thoughts to this, although she sometimes calls him "sweet Sir Toby" she is not as verbally explicit as he is. Rather, let's examine her actions: she banters amicably with Sir Toby constantly, and put a lot of effort into crafting revenge on Malvolio, who for all his faults never insulted her and only weakly threatened her, and she didn't even watch after dropping the letter. Sir Toby did watch though, and was insulted by Malvolio in her presence. It stands to reason, that this 'revenge' was a kind of gift to Sir Toby, and a way to show off her intelligence. Therefore **Maria and Sir Toby's affection may be interpreted as mutual.**

Speaking of her intelligence, let's talk about how well she manages to sound like Olivia, pulling off not just her handwriting but "her very phrases," and writing in verse despite never speaking it. With this letter Maria, in my opinion, pulls off one of the greatest disguises in the play, as **a proletariat successfully impersonating a member of the bourgeoise.** All of the other disguises and transgressions are in a downwards direction on the social hierarchy: the rich Viola to mere page Cesario, her rich brother Sebastion to an unremarkable Roderigo, noble Sir Toby performing like a common drunk. **Maria is the only character to successfully perform *up* the social hierarchy** in order to make a fool out of her superior, and in so doing **challenges the basis of and threatens the ideology of the entire class structure.**

Act 3 Scene 1

On her way to meeting Olivia, Viola meets Feste and crosses wits with the fool on subjects including language and foolery.

If, as discussed in the previous scene's analysis, Fabian's observational actions and lack of love interest make him an ideal reflection of the audience, by the same logic **Feste may be considered a reflection of Shakespeare himself.** He also is not addled by love, and where Fabian observes, Feste is the most skilled "corrupter of words" and (later, *Twelfth Night's* final line) makes the most overtly meta-textual acknowledgement of the entire play. His witticisms and songs are also frequently microcosmic of the play's themes. The performative parallels within the performance are certainly something worth considering.

Omnipotent: all-powerful.

In this particular bout of foolery Feste leads Viola to observe that "the king lies by a beggar, if a beggar dwell near him," and then makes out that this **equalisation of opposite ends of the socio-political class system** was her own argument ("You have said, sir."), when it was in fact a challenge of his assertion to "live by the church." Such ease of linguistic manipulation adds evidence to his representation of an **omnipotent** author. He also touches on **the theme of gender,** wishing not to "make [his] sister wanton" and declaring that marriage makes "fools" of men. Because he makes mockery of both genders equally, he could be considered feminist. Finally, he embodies the theme of disguise in being, as Viola notes, "wise enough to play the fool."

She then comes across Sir Toby and Sir Andrew, the latter of which is impressed by the Viola's courtliness upon greeting Olivia. Olivia bids all her staff leave them, and once alone with Viola she confesses her love. When Viola rejects her, Olivia pretends that she might still grow to love Orsino, in the hopes that Viola will come again on his behalf.

It's odd that he understands French here, whereas he didn't in Act 1 Scene 3 when Sir Toby said "pourquoi." In case you don't speak French and are just dying to know what Sir Andrew and Viola say to each other... my take on that is that no one knows 'why' we are here or why anything happens in this big scary universe (*pourquoi* being the French word for 'why')!

We see more of the **transition into order though imagery** here. The still disguised Viola briefly presents the nautical image of a "voyage," before Olivia orders "the garden gate be shut." The rest of the scene literally plays out within the meticulous order of a walled garden, shutting out the world and wild ocean. Indeed, Olivia initially manages to maintain a level of respectability in this environment, even so far as to notice "the clock" (although not the specific hour) which has long been absent, and also mark the rules of the compass ("there lies your way, due west"). **However, like "the roses of the spring," good sense and propriety are still young within the play's context, and the characters' grips on decorum are still tenuous.**

Tenuous: very weak or slight.

When Viola attempts to leave, Olivia's inhibitions get the better of her. She displays a level of emotional immaturity (begging Cesario to "stay!"), insecurity ("tell me what thou thinks of me"), and wilful blindness ("O [his] scorn looks beautiful") that starkly contrasts her capability in managing household and the scathing wit from her first encounter with 'Cesario.' **Thus, the maddening effect of love is demonstrated**.

Act 3 Scene 2

Sir Andrew wishes to leave Olivia's court, having observed her preferential treatment of Cesario. Sir Toby and Fabian convince him that this is simply her way of seeing whether Sir Andrew will fight for her love, and send him to write a letter challenging Cesario to a duel. Maria fetches them as Malvolio has changed into yellow stockings.

Fabian's story about Olivia truly loving Sir Andrew is very logical and convincing, if, like Sir Andrew, you are blinded by hope and don't have all of the information. This provides an example of how events may be viewed from **multiple perspectives.** Indeed, innumerable different productions have reimagined the text in so many ways, that every reader and audience will take their own perspective too. However, like Fabian, we possess all the information and so are aware that Sir Andrew is just a "manikin" to Sir Toby, but still gleefully participate in his humiliation by reviving the play again and again.

Sir Andrew's response betrays another example of rejection of authority, as "policy [he] hate[s]." **Ironically, in his belief of Toby's smooth assertion that women swoon for valour, he accepts the unwritten societal rules of gender roles while professing to hate strategic written rules of law and civility**.

Valour: bravery.

To add to all of the disguise of the play, Sir Toby bids Sir Andrew to write a letter with "gall in thy ink; though thou write with a goose-pen." 'Gall' refers to boldness and disrespect, and writing with a 'goose-pen' is a roundabout way of calling Sir Andrew a 'goose,' figuratively a foolish person and a coward. So in his letter, Sir Andrew is to seem a cruel and bold individual, while in fact being a foolish coward, just as in her letter Maria appeared the rich and learned Olivia, while in fact being her mere servant. Although, as will be seen, Sir Andrew is not nearly as clever as Maria.

Act 3 Scene 3

Antonio reveals to Sebastian that he stole from Orsino in a battle at sea, and so cannot show him around the city. Instead, he gives Sebastian his purse and they arrange to meet later at an inn.

By Antonio's giving of his purse (and compromising information about being wanted) to Sebastian, we learn that not only does Antonio love him (as discerned from Act 2 Scene 1 and restated here), he also trusts him absolutely.

Sebastian's gentlemanliness is also reinforced, as is his gratitude and wanderlust.

Act 3 Scene 4

Viola has sent after 'Cesario' again, but is distracted by Malvolio's arrival. Olivia assumes that Malvolio, following the ridiculous instructions of Maria's letter, has gone mad and leaves orders for Sir Toby and some of her servants to look after him

Olivia's musings on how best to gain Cesario's love confirm our observation from when she sent him her ring way back in Act 1 Scene 5 – that the more **privileged classes see "youth [as something which] is bought more oft than begged or borrowed," entirely missing the idea that love and trust must be *earned*. The fallacy viewing love as transactional is evident** when, later in the scene, Viola once again refuses Olivia's advances and her gifted "jewel." Shakespeare thus **presents the bourgeoisie as having limited emotional intelligence,** possessed of a worldview **overvaluing money and materialism.**

There is another clue to the class structure of Illyria here that we have not discussed yet, although it is present through the entire play; which **second person singular pronoun** the characters address each other with. **'Thee/thou/thy/thine' etc. is *informal.*** Superiors use it when addressing their subordinates, and friends or family members would use it with each other. **'You' is the *formal* version,** used when speaking to your superior or someone worthy.

When Malvolio starts quoting Maria's letter at Olivia, she doesn't know that he is quoting anything, so she is suitably so shocked when he refers to "thy yellow stockings" and says that "thou art made" (using the *informal* pronoun) that she can only repeat these lines back at him in indignation. Again, Shakespeare's lack of stage directions mean that this could simply be played with bewilderment, but such familiarity from her mere steward implies that he considers her (at best) an equal, if not an inferior, and thus could well inspire anger. **Even in this time of misrule, transgression of the class structure, forgetting one's station in life, is enough to make Malvolio appear "mad" and possessed by evil spirits.**

With Olivia gone, Sir Toby, Maria, and Fabian delight in pretending Malvolio is possessed by Satan. He leaves, still confident in Olivia's love for him, and Sir Andrew arrives with the letter he wrote challenging Cesario to a duel. It's nonsensical, so Sir Toby decides to tell Cesario of the challenge himself.

Again, the potential for **multiple perspectives** is displayed here. **Love for what Olivia represents (a chance to rise above his servile station) blinds Malvolio** to her confusion and allows him to continue finding evidence to support his fantasy, just as it blinds Sir Andrew to her total lack of interest and his manipulation. In driving these and indeed all of the characters to farcical lengths, **love makes them all "mad"** – perceiving reality as different to what it is.

All of the characters that is, except **Feste and Fabian, the puppeteers and observers of the audience's vicarious experience.** Here, there is more evidence of Fabian's symbolism in his **meta-textual** declaration that "if this were played upon a stage now, I could condemn it as improbable fiction." In saying so he reminds the audience that it *is* played upon a stage, and it *is* improbable fiction, **drawing attention to the unreality and theatricality of the performance. Such a distancing tactic shatters the illusion of immersion, forcing us to consciously consider the play and its meaning.**

Vicarious: experienced in the imagination through the actions of another person.

Olivia and Viola enter, Viola attempting unsuccessfully to sway Olivia's ardent love off of herself and onto Orsino. After Olivia leaves, Sir Toby and Fabian corner Viola and convince her that Sir Andrew is very angry with her and deadly in a duel, to which he challenges 'Cesario.' Sir Toby then persuades Sir Andrew that Cesario is equally enraged and skilled in fighting, and the two are manipulated into a sword-fight where each is utterly terrified of the other.

Olivia is aware enough of social norms to understand that both her love of someone below her social class and her actions in pursuing them is a "fault" worth of "reprove." Nevertheless, **she throws herself at 'Cesario' with a vigour and hopeful desperation that, somewhat ironically, parallels that of Malvolio earlier in the scene.** Just as he was deemed to have been possessed by "all the devils of hell" (Sir Toby's words) for his pursuit of Olivia, so she recognises that her actions in the face of Viola's rejection "might bear [her] soul to hell." Similarly, in attempting to impress Olivia, Sir Andrew presents himself as "a devil in private brawl."

The comparison between their uncouth behaviours and hell goes to show how strongly against society such 'misrule' is, hell being the **chaotic and horrifying opposite to the biblical image of what is good and right.** Thus, the characters' actions during this time and the conclusions that might be drawn from them (i.e. that anything is permissible in the name of love, that all are equal in the face of love, etc.) are the *exact opposite* of what is actually presented as good and right. **This play is comical because it shows its audience how *not* to be.**

These scene shows one such transgression – that of gender norms – quite clearly. **Neither Olivia nor Sir Andrew embody traditional femininity or masculinity,** given Olivia's stubbornness (shown both in her steadfast and overt refusal of Orsino's suit and her unswayable pursuit of Cesario) and Sir Andrew's **impotence.**

Impotence: helplessness or inability to take effective action.

This failure to match society's image of the demure woman and strong man is highlighted in contrast to the images the present of themselves, which *do* fit these moulds; Olivia presents Viola with her picture which "hath no tongue to vex [her]," and Sir Andrew is portrayed (within his wishes) as "bloody as the hunter." This shows an awareness of societal expectations, even as they go unfulfilled.

Viola and Sir Andrew's duel is interrupted by the arrival of Antonio who, mistaking Viola for her brother Sebastian, demands to fight in her place. Sir Toby and Antonio fight, but they are also interrupted when the police arrive to arrest Antonio for his crimes at sea. He asks Viola to return his purse (still thinking that she is Sebastian) and is heartbroken that 'Sebastian' 'pretends' not to recognise him.

Antonio asks for no context before jumping into this fight. He doesn't seem to care how skilled his opponents are, or whether or not Sebastian brought this duel upon himself. **The lack of conditions on the assertion that he will fight can be seen as a metaphor for Antonio's unconditional love for Sebastian.** Unlike previously in this scene, such extreme action isn't called madness or compared to hell. On the contrary, Antonio's line "vile an idol proves this god" implies that prior to this apparent betrayal, he considered Sebastian a "god," whereas now is "o'er-flourished by the devil." In addition, it is only after said 'betrayal' that officer 1 says Antonio "grows mad", in reference to his ranting about Sebastian's cruel recompense for his love, not in reference to the sword fight. This adds depth to the previous comparisons of love, madness, and hell; **only unrequited love is considered evil, while love that is shared is the purest form of goodness in existence.**

Unrequited: not returned.

Antonio's love was so pure it even shirked the expectations of capitalism. His love for Sebastian was based on "**venerable** worth," (rather than monetary worth) and he freely gave away his purse. However, his uniqueness in this matter is contrasted against the capitalism of society in which money is a "necessity."

Venerable: worthy of respect because of one's age, wisdom, or character.

Once again we see the **power of perspective,** with Viola's offer to give *half* of her (already "low" amount of) money to a stranger really quite generous. But from Antonio's perspective, it is a cruel trick of Sebastian's to thieve the majority of his own purse.

Viola's remark, "I hate ingratitude more in a man" than anything else, matches her brother's gratefulness to Antonio in the previous scene ("thanks, / And thanks, and ever thanks"). This shows their similarity in more than just appearance. It also in some way forgives herself, Sir Toby and Orsino their flaws of "lying, vainness, babbling drunkenness," respectively, thus **creating a didactic** moral code for the audience. Key to this code, as well as gratitude, is kindness. This is reinforced in this scene, as in others, though the theme of the inner verses the outer version of a person: "in nature there's no blemish but the mind: / None can be called deformed but the unkind." Thus, **exterior facades including beauty, status, even disguise, are ultimately less important than who you are on the inside.**

Didactic: designed to teach, or provide moral or ethical lessons, instructions, or guidance.

Viola begins to suspect and hope that her brother is still alive. When she leaves, Sir Toby and Fabian egg on Sir Andrew to follow and finish the duel that was started. As there is **goodness in mutual love,** Viola here recognises that there is **truth in passion.** This is consistent with her own slip-ups over the course of the play, mentioning her true female identity in moments of animation or desire (e.g. "I am all the daughters of my father's house" in Act 2 Scene 4). We also see an atypical reference to the ocean with *positive* connotations, in Viola's hope that "tempests are kind, and salt waves fresh in love." **Thus, the tide of wild revelry begins to turn, and the melancholy of love to transform into benevolence.**

Act 4 Scene 1

Feste mocks Sebastian for not recognising him, mistaking him for Cesario. Sir Andrew, Sir Toby, and Fabian arrive, and all make the same mistake about Sebastian's identity. Sir Andrew hits him, and Sebastian is quick to fight back, finding himself about to duel Sir Toby when Olivia arrives. She also believes Sebastian is Cesario, calls off the fight and apologises to him profusely. Sebastian is both confused and delighted by her adoration, and agrees to go with her. **Feste's foolery to Sebastian mocks the class system,** impersonating someone of status at least equal to that of Sebastian himself (denoted in his use of the informal "thou" where before he used "you") while using overly pretentious language in bidding him "ungird thy strangeness," thus **presenting the upper echelons as overly pretentious.**

Echelon: a level/rank of an organisation or of society.

The class system is still, nevertheless, very present. Indeed, paired with Antonio's desperation for money when arrested in the last scene, Sir Andrew's confidence that he can successfully sue 'Cesario' for **battery** despite the fact that Sir Andrew "struck him first" **implies that in Illyria, the law serves the wealthy instead of justice.** The subtlety of this implication evidences just how implicit within society this assumption is; it does not need to be spelled out.

Battery: in this context, this means physical assault.

Once Olivia does break up the fight, she fully displays her power (in commanding Sir Toby and friends to leave, and being immediately obeyed), and assertiveness (in *telling* Sebastian to "go with me" rather than asking demurely), **in contravention of the traditionally submissive feminine role.** Indeed, her act of breaking up the fight itself is an **inversion of the 'hero-swooping-in-to-save-the-damsel' trope.** And Sebastian *likes* this atypical relationship dynamic, agreeing to "be ruled by" her (in contrast to Orsino's wish to be her "King" at the expense of "all affections else" in Act 1 Scene 1). This presents a strong argument for those of you looking at feminist critical perspectives; **the presentation and acceptance of assertive female characters may be considered didactic.** Remember though, before suggesting that the play is feminist, that **there are only three female characters in the play, compared to eleven male characters.**

> **Key Point :**
> When writing an essay from a critical perspective, **remember to address all aspects.** For example, when exploring a Marxist perspective remember to analyse the presentation of both the proletariat *and* the bourgeoisie. Likewise, given that feminism is about the equality of the sexes, remember to consider the presentation of both women *and* men. Is one social class or gender presented more positively/negatively, or more fully/one-dimensionally than the other?

Finally, there are a couple of moments of **dramatic irony** to look at here. Feste's statement that "nothing that is so is so," reminds the audience of the **innumerable levels of disguise and trickery** within the play, and Sebastian's wondering "Are all the people mad?" hearkens back to our analysis of the last scene when we decided that pretty much, yep. Everyone is mad from unrequited love. Sebastian even succumbs to such "mad[ness]" himself when presented with the adoration and tender affections of a total stranger (Olivia).

Act 4 Scene 2

Curate: basically a Christian pastor.

At Maria's request, Feste disguises himself as "Sir Topas the **curate**" to further torment Malvolio, who has been locked in a dark room and treated as though he were demonically possessed. Sir Toby decides he has had enough fun with him and wishes the game were over, leaving with Maria to his chamber. Feste removes his disguise and speaks with Malvolio as himself, and eventually agrees to bring him paper, pen, and light so that he may write to Olivia.

At last! Feste is in disguise, meaning that now *every single* significant character (i.e. excluding Valentine and Curio) has lied to or mislead another for their own gain or enjoyment. If there was ever any doubt, it is now irrefutable that **disguise is a major theme** of this play.

While in disguise Feste contradicts his statement from last scene ("nothing that is so is so") in saying "that that is, is." This shows both an understanding that nothing perceived as reality within the play can be trusted, and simultaneously a willingness to bend the realities of others for entertainment, hypocritically **encouraging gullibility while being a critical thinker** himself. Feste also hides meaning behind clever words. For example, his assertion that the "bay windows [are as] transparent as barricadoes" leads Malvolio to believe that there is light in his prison and he is mad to see darkness, when in fact "barricadoes" are fortifications filled with earth and stones and so Feste is in fact agreeing that it is dark. He uses the truth to lie, and twists words with more mastery than any other character. **This mastery over language contributes evidence to the 'Feste as authorial representation' theory, omniscient and omnipotent within the play.**

There are two songs in this scene, both designed to reflect the situation and torment Malvolio. The first, 'Hey Robin, jolly Robin', is about a man who's "lady... loves another," just like Malvolio (who, like the song, has always called Olivia "my lady"). The other song, 'I am gone, sir,' requires a little more unpacking to make sense of.

Lyrics	Meaning
I am gone, sir And anon, sir I'll be with you again	Feste is leaving Malvolio, and will return soon.
In a trice Like to the old Vice You need to sustain	The "old Vice" was a character in morality plays. He was the devil's son, who carried a flimsy and harmless wooden dagger, and was a predecessor of the Elizabethan fool. Thus, with "Vice" Feste (being a fool) is referring to himself. So he's saying, I'll be back "in a trice," just like how long you (Malvolio) took to turn to me (the fool, old Vice) with your need to affirm your sanity. We see as the play goes on that Feste actually takes a long while to pass Malvolio's letter to Olivia, prolonging Malvolio's suffering, which makes sense in this context because for a long time Malvolio hated the fool. Only now (almost four fifths through the play) does he treat Feste with respect and call him "good fool."
Who, with dagger of lath, In his rage and his wrath, Cries, 'Ah ha' to the devil, Like a mad lad, 'Pare thy nails, dad?'	Given all of the previous imagery around madness and hell, it is logical for "the devil" to refer to Malvolio. Ironically, in morality plays Vice was the devil's son, and so Feste offers a mocking respect, posing Malvolio as a father figure, while also suggesting that they're more alike than the puritanical Malvolio would like to believe. Just as Vice offered the devil a flimsy wooden dagger (lath is a very thin, flat strip of wood) to trim his nails, so Feste fetches Malvolio tools (pen, paper, light) which may not be sufficient for the task. In this case, proving Malvolio's sanity.
Adieu, goodman devil.	Feste leaves, finishing the song and also saying goodbye to Malvolio.

Beyond the deeper meanings that can be analysed from the songs lyrics, there is also the simple fact that **Feste is tormenting Malvolio,** who has been described on multiple occasions as a Puritan (Puritans were anti-music), with song.

Act 4 Scene 3

Sebastian, still glad for but bewildered by Olivia's love, tries to use logic and reason to decide whether or not he is mad. Deciding that reality is what one makes of it, he agrees to go with her to be married.

Olivia's final gift to the man she believes to be Cesario – and which Sebastian uses to prove to himself his own sanity – is a pearl. The **symbolism** of this arises from the contrast to the cruel crashing waves of the ocean that have previously been evoked; in that **a clam was battered around by the hungry ocean, as all of the characters have been battered by the madness of misrule and love, yet were still able to create something beautiful.** Furthermore, this scene takes place in Olivia's garden. As previously mentioned, **the increasing use of garden imagery is a metaphor for the growth of meticulous order and harmony out of the chaos of misrule and madness.**

All of **this transitional imagery matches Olivia's "haste" to leave behind madness and instability in favour of the rules and structure of marriage,** now that 'Cesario' appears to share her feelings. And before you judge him for marrying a woman he just met, remember that **time within this play is ambiguous.** We know that enough time has passed for her to give him a gift, arrange a priest to marry them, and for him to observe her "sway her house, [and] command her followers." Indeed, as madness has been established to befall only those plagued with unrequited love**, Sebastian's decision that he is "not mad..." suggests that he does love Olivia in return.**

She, for her part, also **begins to return to the rules of the class system,** planning for the kind of marriage "celebration" that would be expected by someone of her stature ("according to my birth").

The scene (and Act 4) ends with Olivia and Sebastian presenting a rhyming couplet each. Structurally, the use of rhyme and metre matches the thematic return to predefined conventions, and Sebastian's declaration that "having sworn truth, ever will be true" demonstrates a commitment to this change.

Act 5 Scene 1

This entire act is one long scene, so buckle in!

Feste has Malvolio's letter to Olivia and refuses to let Fabian see it. Orsino arrives with Viola and other (unnamed) attendants and after giving Feste some money for his witty fooling, sends him away to fetch Olivia. Antonio is brought before them, and recounts how he saved and spent three months at sea with Sebastian (implying that is it Viola), but Orsino counters that this is impossible as Viola has been his own servant for the last three months.

Feste's possession of Malvolio's letter and withholding of it from Fabian is a wonderful display of their **symbolic representation of the author and audience**, respectively; Feste (as omniscient 'author') knows what is yet to occur in the play, and Fabian (as the audience) wants to know but must wait until Feste deems it the right time.

Further to Feste's wit, in his foolery with Orsino the fool claims to be an ass and in so doing ironically proves himself to be quite clever. Thus, the **juxtaposition of what one purports to be against what one actually is in reality** is once again highlighted, and so the theme of 'inner v. outer' remains in play. As you might expect, most of the key themes rear their ugly heads in this scene, as it is **the climax and denouement** of the entire play.

Orsino arrives with a number of unnamed attendants, who don't have any dialogue and so are not really characters. These individuals' only purpose is to **provide a visual representation of Orsino's status and power.** It would seem, therefore, that his ego remains as enormous as ever. Indeed, even in describing the objectively awful scenario of a sea battle, he **maintains poetic use of hyperbolic metaphors and evocative imagery** ("[Antonio's] face... besmeared... in the smoke of war"), and speaks, as always, in verse. Other characters tend to favour verse or prose depending on their status, but do move between them. His **exclusive use of verse shows his position on the extreme end of the class (and conceit) spectrum.**

Conceit: excessive pride in oneself.

And time is officially no longer ambiguous! **For the first time since Viola began working for Orsino, the elapsed time since she washed ashore is stated explicitly and specifically: three months.** Thus, within the first few minutes of the final Act, we have returned unambiguously to the rule of social class, and of time.

Olivia arrives and is shocked to see Cesario attending to Orsino, having just (so she believes) married him. Orsino is upset (to put it lightly) by Olivia's constant rejection, and suspecting her love for Cesario, he threatens to kill Viola out of spite. When Viola announces that she loves Orsino more than anything in the world and goes after Orsino willing to die for him if he so wishes, Olivia summons the priest and reveals (to Orsino's dismay) that Cesario is her husband.

Orsino's reaction to first seeing Olivia implies that he is still in (his own selfish semblance of) love with her, saying "here comes the countess; now heaven walks on earth." But, only three lines later, he has turned to describing her as an "uncivil lady... ingrate and **unauspicious**." This rapid change, prompted by Olivia's continued rejection, demonstrates Orsino's **lack of character growth.** As with music in the very first scene, he is temperamentally liable to move from adoration to dismissal very quickly, and possessed of a deep-seated conviction that he is owed a woman's total devotion. Similarly, Viola has not become any less passive or likely to blame the supernatural, as shown in her lack of attempt to engage with Sebastian until he speaks to her first, and her initial assumption that he is a ghost. Equally, Olivia is as active and against pretension and ceremony as ever, having unceremoniously eloped with a Sebastian. Indeed, in my opinion there has been little, if any, growth in any of the characters' personalities or beliefs. This could **reflect the superficiality of the play as a comedy, and/or demonstrate the purpose of licensed misrule; to allow an outlet for difference in order to ultimately entrench the status quo.**

Inauspicious: not promising, or unlikely to suceed.

Status quo: the existing state of affairs, particularly concerning social or political norms.

On the other hand, you may say that because of Viola's disguise Orsino has learned to "tender dearly" a woman for her individuality and wit, rather than for her superficial appearance. Or that Viola *has* learned to actively pursue what she wants, given her declaration of love for Orsino even while still disguised.

KEY POINT :
You may find evidence for the development of some or all characters. Remember that this book is only a starting place, a suggestion of ideas. **Interpret the text as you will, reaching whatever conclusion makes the most sense to you or most contributes to your analysis of the play as a whole.**

Indeed, one of the themes in *Twelfth Night* is the existence of **multiple perspectives. This theme is reinforced** by Orsino's perception of Olivia as having a heart of stone ("marble breasted tyrant"), while from her point of view she is as full of love as a person could be, just not for him. **The recurrent motif of disparity between ones inner and outer selves is also reiterated** with Orsino's depiction of Olivia as a "dove" with a "raven's heart."

Sir Andrew and Sir Toby arrive, wounded from another fight they picked with Sebastian. They leave to see a doctor. Sebastian arrives and apologises to Olivia for hurting them, especially so soon after their wedding. Everyone watching is completely gobsmacked because Sebastian and Viola are in the same room, and they look completely identical.

The twins hesitantly question each other to confirm their identities, and Viola says that if her disguise hinders Sebastian's recognition of her, she can retrieve her female clothes from the Sea Captain that saved her. It becomes clear that Olivia married Sebastian after falling in love with Viola, disguised as Cesario. Orsino realises that Viola, in disguise, has often confessed her love for him.

Olivia remembers that Malvolio has supposedly gone mad. Feste produces his letter but, because he insists on reading it in a mad voice, Olivia gives it to Fabian to read. The letter proves he is not insane, and Olivia sends Fabian to bring him to them. Meanwhile, Orsino announces that he will marry Viola.

Now that the social order is reinstating itself, Sir Toby appears to be losing his sense of identity. He thrived more than the other characters in an environment of unrestrained mischief, revelry, and manipulation, to the extent that he may well represent the **'Lord of Misrule'** (see page 5). Now, that world is crumbling around him and he finds himself no longer amused by Sir Andrew, insulting him to the extent where he is unlikely to be able to continue manipulating him, and professes to "hate a drunken rogue." **This is ironic, as he is drunk himself, but also potentially an indicator of self-loathing, driving away the only person who he could really consider a friend. Later we learn that he has married Maria – two of the most socially transgressive characters in the play start anew in a relationship governed by the strict law of tradition.** Perhaps this displays, more poignantly than anything else, the **return to social order.**

One aspect of this return, is **the reinstatement of status according to gender.** This is clearest in Orsino's release of Viola from service, citing that the work of a page is "so much against the **mettle** of your sex." This **implies that women are more delicate and fragile than men, less capable.** More symbolically, although Maria, Olivia, and Viola's **actions during the plot may have been empowered and shown agency and intelligence, but now their voices are silenced.** Orsino once declared "give me thy hand... you shall from this time be your master's mistress," but Viola literally does not speak for the rest of the Act. Olivia, once she realises she has married a stranger, ceases her (previously very vocal) adorations of her husband and is very empathetic to the "notorious abuse" suffered by Malvolio, possibly out of empathy from her own position of having been mislead in love. As for Maria, she hasn't even made an onstage appearance since Act 4 Scene 2. **Furthermore, the contrast in language used to discuss feminine and masculine objects shows a clear distaste for the former.** Viola's male clothes are described as "attire" – connoting formality and fine craftsmanship – whereas her female clothes are called "weeds" – connoting feebleness and inferiority – thus reflecting the societal expectations of men and women more generally.

Mettle: the ability to cope with difficult situations.

Another aspect of the return to social norms is the **emphasis on binary gender and heteronormativity.** It could be argued that during the 'misrule' period of the play, Viola's disguise presented an exploration of non-binary gender, Orsino's attraction to her in the belief that she was male created homoerotic tensions, and Olivia's love may have belied attraction to feminine or **androgynous** qualities. This is particularly notable when analysing the play from a Queer Critical Perspective, in consideration of the idea that gender is performative rather than innate (especially remembering that the original actors were all men, including for the female characters) and a societal construction. Thus, **in the emphasis in this final act on marriage between men and women, most notably in Orsino's refusal to marry Viola until she is dressed as a woman, the previously suggested spectrum of gender expression and sexual attraction is eradicated.**

Heteronormative: normalisation of male-female relationships and heterosexuality over other relationships and sexual orientations.

Androgynous: ambiguous in gender appearance.

Finally, **classism also returns. In addition explicate references to nobility and class,** such as Orsino's assurance that Sebastian is a worthy husband to Olivia because "right noble is his blood," and that Viola's work as a servant was "so far beneath [her] soft and tender breeding," **there are also structural cues.** As previously mentioned, **Orsino makes a grand display of power** through the onstage attendants, consistent with his privilege as the most noble (and also the *rich*est *man*) in the play. He also has the final word of the play (not counting Feste's song because it's a *song*, because Feste is alone onstage when he sings it, and because Feste's words and actions throughout the play place him outside of all the rules of society and in some ways the bounds of the play. More on that later!). **Inversely, Maria, being the antithesis of Orsino as a common servant woman, is utterly absent.**

Antithesis: absolute opposite.

Malvolio arrives and confronts Olivia with the letter he found in the garden. It becomes evident that it is a forgery, and Fabian and Feste confess the trick that they played. Fabian mentions that Sir Toby married Maria because she so cleverly planned their practical joke and wrote the letter, and Feste admits that he joined in as revenge for Malvolio's criticism of his fooling at the very start of the play. Malvolio leaves, vowing to get revenge on them all, and Orsino sends after him to get Viola's clothes for their wedding.

As Fabian and Feste confess to their tricking of Malvolio, **the final disguise of the play is lifted.** With social order now restored, let's look at the final fate of the characters to see who won. Because despite all the love and marriage, it certainly isn't 'happily every after.'

Malvolio loses. Olivia promises that he will be "both plaintiff and the judge" in order to see justice served when the perpetrators come to light, but this promise is broken. The steward has lost his dignity, his hope for love, and his authority. **Why? From a meta-textual perspective,** Feste's triumph over Malvolio could **represent the triumph of theatre over puritanism**, a kind of catharsis for Shakespeare and an easy villain for the theatre-loving audience. **From a Marxist perspective,** perhaps he is being 'punished' for his **hubris in seeking to wed well above his social station,** and although moved by passion to speak in verse, that is as close as he will get to the dominion of the upper classes.

Hubris: excessive pride and self-confidence; in Greek tragedies this referred to the prideful defiance of the gods, leading to a character's punishment.

Sir Andrew and Antonio also lose. Sir Andrew has been manipulated out of his money, been rejected by his only friend, and rejected by Olivia whose love he sought. Antonio has also lost his money, suffered emotional trauma, and is left facing jail or bankruptcy while his best friend who he loves (but has never professed to love him in return) marries and ascends to a social status that is way out of his own circles of association. **Why? From a feminist perspective,** perhaps they are being 'punished' for **embodying versions of masculinity that do not align with the traditional,** socially acceptable version; Sir Andrew is an idiot and a coward, Antonio is too emotionally expressive, and they were both too trusting with their money and friendship. **Contrast this to Sebastian and Orsino.**

Orsino *mostly* wins. He does end up married to a beautiful and eligible woman, one who he has grown to cherish for more than her beauty and who adores him in return. **This corresponds with his unbelievably high status as a Duke, and a rich, intelligent man.** But he doesn't get what he wanted, the hand of Olivia, who is more powerful and more noble than Viola and therefore (by the sexist and imperialist societal valuation system of Illyria) a greater 'prize'. Why? **Perhaps this slight sting can be attributed to his fickle overemotional personality, that slightly lowers his status by not adhering to the patriarchal definition of ideal masculinity** (unlike Sebastian).

Similarly to Orsino, **Olivia *sort of* wins.** Corresponding with her wealth and position as a countess, she is lucky enough to marry Sebastian who is basically a good guy. But in marriage, she has (according to the laws and norms of the time) given away control over her wealth, her estate, and herself, essentially to a stranger. However nice Sebastian may be, she is condemned to give up her independence to someone that she did not fall in love with. Why? **From a feminist critical perspective,** perhaps because she was **too powerful for a woman.** Because her father and brother died, she controlled an entire estate, and in seeking to retain this power by marrying someone below her station, **she presented a tangible threat to the structure of the male hegemony.** By having her marry a noble who she did not love, this threat was neutralised.

Sir Toby and Maria, as discussed previously, lose their place in the world, but win each other. The first time I read that they got married, it felt like it came out of the blue. But on subsequent read-throughs I noticed more and more clues to their relationship that I have tried to highlight here. Consequently, this ending for them seems mostly positive.

Viola gets what she wants, but this is hardly a win from a modern standpoint. She marries Orsino, the man that she has loved since the play's beginning, and will live a life of endless riches and privilege as his Duchess/Countess. Her brother is saved as well, so **all her dreams come true.** This corresponds with Viola's contrasting personality to Olivia; despite disguising herself as a male, her **passivity and constant affirmation of her femininity** in asides to the audience mean that she was **never truly a threat to the patriarchy.** She simply transferred the domestic servitude and adoration for a husband expected of a female, into 'male' servitude and adoration for a master. Hence, the favourable outcome. However, like all three women of the play, she is still married and thereby (according to the oppressive laws of the time) **loses her independence and submits to oppression.**

Sebastian wins the grand prize. He was rescued from drowning, finds his sister alive and well, and the most beautiful and powerful woman in the country has thrown herself at him for marriage. His outcome is objectively the best as he improves all of his initial prospects (death, grief, and a good name but no estate or wealth). **Why? Because he embodies the epitome of the status quo's 'ideal,' seen through any perspective:**

- **Feminism:** he hides his emotions (as seen in Act 2 Scene 1), is intelligent and guided by logic (speaks in verse and uses logical reasoning to decide whether he is mad in Act 4 Scene 3), is quick and skilful in a fight (injures Sir Toby and Sir Andrew without getting a scratch himself), is honourable and loyal (only engages in the aforementioned fight for his own safety, then apologises to Olivia), modest and attractive (says that Viola is beautiful but discounts his own looks despite being identical), and decisive (quickly agrees to marry Olivia).
- **Marxism:** he is of noble birth and adheres to the decorum that is therefore expected of him, treating individuals of lower classes with respect yet commanding a superiority that leads him to leave Antonio and bid him not follow (Act 2 Scene 1) and to similarly send away Feste (Act 4 Scene 1).
- **Queer Theory:** he never disguises himself as anything other than a man, never shows romantic interest in anyone other than the (very feminine) woman Olivia.

Psychoanalytics: a critical perspective that argues that literary texts, like dreams, express the secret unconscious desires and anxieties. In psychoanalysis, the three sections of Freud's (disfavoured by modern psychologists) structural model of the human psyche are often discussed: the id (primitive and selfish instincts), the superego (moral consciousness) and the ego (balance between the two).

- **Psychoanalytical/Freudian Theory:** he is in total balance of his own id (in caving to his selfish want to marry Olivia) and superego (in doing everything he *should* do according to society, listed above) as an individual, and is also a symbol of the superego as a 'perfect' character within Illyria, whose arrival coincides with the other characters leaving their id-centric period of misrule to return to the balance of the ego.

Thus, Sebastian's favourable treatment by Shakespeare in the plot's ending, in contrast to the fates of all the other characters, can be seen as an endorsement of his qualities. Thereby, **the patriarchy, class system, and heteronormative attitudes,** and neurotypical privilege, and the status quo behind any other critical perspective you want to apply. There are loads of them. **that support such qualities may also be considered endorsed by this play.** However, that is not to say that Shakespeare endorsed them. Perhaps, he was simply portraying the world with honesty, as he saw it to be.

As for Feste and Fabian, nothing really changes for them. **Feste is still free to play the fool, Fabian fades back into Olivia (and now Sebastian's) service. This aligns with their existence outside of the normal rules of the play:** Feste acknowledges the strange "whirligig of time," and his final song implies a knowledge stretching back to its very beginnings, and beyond the confines of the play. Fabian has "wondered at" the events, and even assisted Sir Toby in his manipulations, but never been caught up in them on his own.

Everyone leaves the stage except Feste, who sings one last song to end the play. *Twelfth Night* is the only Shakespeare play which both begins and ends with music. This may be because music, like the fleeting misrule of the play, is transitory. Indeed, most of Feste's songs revolve around the themes of temporality of life, youth, and even love. And this final song is no exception.

The second and forth lines of each verse (apart from the last one) are repeated, "With hey, ho, the wind and the rain... For the rain it raineth every day." The recurrence of the wild whether motif presents **a pathetic fallacy that aligns not with the happy return to social order, but with sadness and uncontrollable anger, thus implying the difficulty of life under stringent convention of society.**

The progression of the verses shows the chronological stages of a man's life, from being "a little tiny boy" to being a "drunken" old man ("came unto my beds" has been interpreted by some scholars, including James Orchard Halliwell-Phillipps, in accordance with a passage from *Characters* – written by Thomas Overbury in 1615 – which equates 'leaving at breakfast' with dying as an infant, 'leaving at dinner' with dying during youth, and 'leaving at bedtime' with dying in old age). The final verse breaks this pattern, juxtaposing one man's short life against the timeline of the entire world, and one fictional representation of a man in a song against the vast reality beyond the world of the play. That's right, Feste knows that he is in a play. What's more, however much we may analyse, it would appear that in Feste's opinion, the play's only meaning or purpose was an attempt to "please" us, its audience.

Section 4

Character Analysis

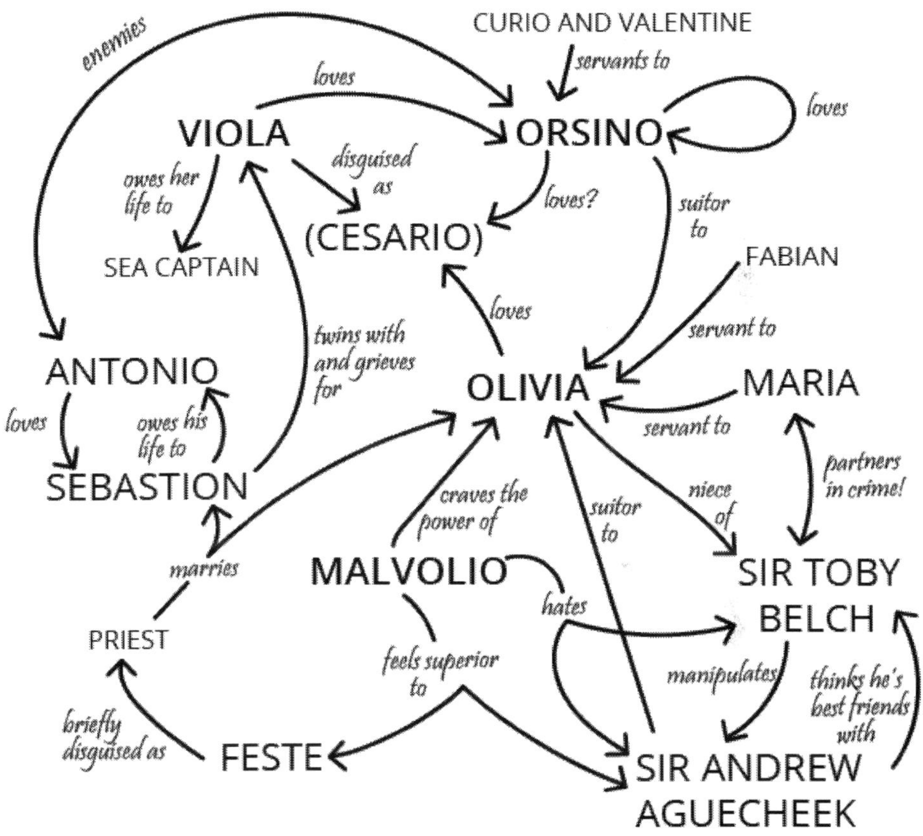

Orsino

Orsino is a very powerful nobelman in Illyria who wants to marry the Countess Olivia despite her steadfast rejection of his attempts to woo her. However, just how powerful he is remains uncertain. Until Act 1 Scene 4 he is consistently called a 'duke', but after this he is referred to as a 'count' by the other characters while still being a duke according to the stage directions. If he is a count, then he is on an equal footing in terms of status and political influence as Olivia; if he is a duke then he is significantly more important. Why the confusion? Some scholars believe that the source for *Twelfth Night* was in fact Shakespeare's last draft of the play, known as 'foul papers,' and thus is riddled with mistakes and inaccuracies.

From the beginning, we see a few of his character traits stand out. Firstly, we have his **moodiness.** Orsino is highly temperamental. Shakespeare establishes this in his very first monologue, in which he very quickly turns from wanting "excess" of music, to flippantly declaring "no more." Shakespeare even draws attention to this particular example by ending with a rhyming couplet. Later, Feste observes that Orsino has an "opal" mind, referring to how quickly he changes his opinion like an opal changing colour under the light. He also contradicts himself in his argument with Cesario about whether men or women are better lovers, and even at the very end rebounds astonishingly quickly from 'loving' Olivia more than anything in the world, to hating her, to deciding to marry Viola, and then liking Olivia again as a "sweet sister." Thus, with regards to this trait, there is **no character growth.**

Purports: claims to do something.

Orsino is also remarkably **egotistic** – although he **purports** to love Olivia, it's pretty clear that he's only in love with the idea of love itself, a narcissistic fantasy of his own making. He has no respect or empathy for the fact that Olivia's *brother just died*, and all of his moping about how in love he is centres around himself; *his* melancholy, *his* devotion, how much she will worship *him* as his wife, rather than the qualities for which he has supposedly fallen in love with her. Indeed, the **superficiality of his 'love'** shows itself in the fact that the only real complements he manages to muster for Olivia are all about her beauty, showing no knowledge or interest in her as a person. **Once again, this trait doesn't much develop throughout the play;** Orsino declares himself the epitome of "all lovers" to Cesario in Act 2 and believing himself to have more passion than any woman could, then in the final Act throws a total tantrum when he doesn't get what he wants (Olivia).

Orsino is also a massive, **melodramatic** drama queen! In the above mentioned tantrum, Orsino actually threatens to *murder* Cesario, who he really quite likes, because he is "jealous." And while his poetry about Olivia is lovely in terms of cadence and range of reference, showing his education, it is also riddled with repetitive clichés and extreme images that show how much he loves to exaggerate. For example, his first speech trods the well-worn and highly unoriginal poetic path of comparing love to music and flowers, and the extremes to which he takes these images – "a dying fall... [a] sweet sound" that **belie** an addiction to melancholy.

Belie: to give a misleading or contradictory impression (e.g. a smiling face might belie or hide someone's deep suffering).

So basically, Orsino is a fully grown, rich and powerful man who behaves like a self-absorbed, foot-stomping child, screaming for a different shiny thing every five minutes. Clearly, **Shakespeare has designed this character to be humorous, and uses Orsino's antics to poke fun at the upper classes.** But he's not a totally lost cause; Viola falls in love with him!

Even before he knows that she is a woman, Orsino finds a trust for 'Cesario' that emboldens him to favour Viola over his other servants, and share with her "his secret soul." Perhaps this is because **she challenges his egotistical assumptions at every turn,** trying to make him respect Olivia's rejection of him, and defending womens' ability to love.

In doing so, she also reveals to him her own 'secret soul,' albeit under disguise. There is also a chemical attraction, as Viola clearly finds Orsino handsome and even before her disguise is lifted he appreciates her own beauty, rather sensuously describing her "lip... smooth and rubious." **Thus, although he has not grown as an *individual* by the end of the play, in his relationship with Viola there is potential for her to temper and transform him into a better man.**

So that's great for Orsino, but I still don't understand what Viola sees in him. **The idea that her entire purpose is to improve him certainly contravenes modern feminist ideologies,** but then again Shakespeare is neither modern nor a definitive feminist, so these are aspects of Orsino's character that you can critically examine.

Curio and Valentine

I'm analysing these two together because Curio and Valentine are very minor characters. As servants to Orsino, **their presence serves to show the audience that Orsino is rich and wealthy.**

Curio has four lines, all of which merely prompt Orsino to begin another melancholy declaration. His first line, "Will you go hunt, my lord?" shows an attempt to bring Orsino out of his slump, suggesting that he has been languishing for Olivia for some time. His other lines serve merely to further the plot.

Valentine has three lines, and all of them are **pure exposition,** like the fact that Olivia rejects Orsino's suit, and that Orsino favours Viola. It is interesting that **he speaks in verse, in contrast to Olivia's servants, and this demonstrates that Orsino has a more pretentious house than Viola,** and makes even his servants adhere to pompous standards of decorum.

Exposition: explanation of background information

Although Curio and Valentine barely qualify as fully fledged characters in their own rights, **we learn more about Orsino by the way they interact with him. Thus Shakespeare skilfully manipulates the theatrical medium** such that within the very first scene the audience is informed of Orsino's power and attitude.

Viola

Viola is an aristocrat who washes up on Illyria's shore and disguises herself as a man called 'Cesario' in order to become Orsino's servant. He sends her to woo Olivia on his behalf, and her disguise prevents her from telling Orsino that she has fallen in love with him, or telling Olivia why she cannot love her back when the countess falls in love with 'Cesario.'

Viola's cross-dressing causes most of the play's shenanigans, but why does she do it? **From a purely logical perspective, having washed ashore with no money, she needed a job;** Olivia wasn't taking applications (because of her recently dead brother,) and while she *could* have been a female domestic servant for Orsino, it would have been harder work with less pay. **From a more emotionally aware standpoint, she is buying herself some time** to play pretend, before having to be "delivered to the [real] world" in which her twin brother is dead. **In this way she is similar to Olivia,** who also shuts herself off from the world to mourn, unable or unwilling to confront a reality without her brother.

Whatever her motivation, **Viola's disguise has serious implications for the themes and commentary of the play** as much as it does for the plot. **It blurs the line of binary gender** and shows that androgyny can be attractive. **It suggests that gender may be performative** rather than innate, as she is accepted as a male simply for dressing and performing the social role of one. **It suggests that the divide between classes may also be performative,** given that her actions as a servant prevent other characters from seeing her as a noble. **And it suggests that given the opportunity, women are equal to men in capability.**

Counterintuitively, in light of these rather progressive implications, **her social transgression (dressing as a man) ultimately causes the consummation of heterosexual marriages that reaffirm both the patriarchy and class system.** These societal structures were threatened by Olivia's power as the head of her noble household and refusal to marry up, Sir Toby's fraternisation with servants, and Orsino's being so lovelorn and shut in at his castle that he wasn't exercising his rule over the county/dukedom. But Viola's 'Cesario' pulls both Olivia and Orsino out of their self-absorbed states, in giving Orsino a relationship grounded in trust and reality rather than fantasy and egoism, and tempting Olivia out of her avowed seven years of mourning.

However, this wasn't all part of some great pro-authority master plan. On the contrary, **Viola's actions are largely driven by passivity and naivety.** Although her choice to disguise her gender and identity could be considered proactive and bold, her **inability to deal with its consequences** when things get complicated – instead leaving her problems up to "fate" and "time" to solve – show instead that it was impulsive and not well thought through. Perhaps she, Olivia, and Orsino all simply want what they cannot have.

Key Point :
To Olivia, Cesario represents youth, freedom, and is a suitor that won't cost her her independence. To Viola, Orsino represents her old, noble-born life. For Orsino, Olivia's love would validate his own inflated self-image. (This interpretation also holds for other characters: Malvolio wants Olivia's status, and Sir Andrew wants her respect.)

Sea Captain

The nameless Sea Captain rescued Viola from drowning, informs her about the state of affairs in Illyria, and assists her in disguising herself as Cesario. Like other relatively minor characters Curio and Valentine, **his primary purposes are to provide the audience with relevant exposition and an illumination of a major character (Viola) via an interaction, and to enable the continuation of the plot.** His education, evident in his speaking in verse, associates Viola with learned individuals, and his assumption of the lower status in the relationship by seeking to please her, accepting her gold, and answering her questions serves to boost hers.

Viola notes that the Sea Captain has a "mind that suits [his] fair and outward character." Thus, his presence is also used to present one of the key themes of the play: the contrast between one's inner and outer self.

After Act 1 Scene 2, the Sea Captain makes no more appearances in the play. **This 'disappearance' of a man whose inner and outer selves are the same coincides with Viola's concealment of her true 'inner' self and indeed much more widespread disguise and deception throughout the play.**

Thus, Shakespeare once again uses a minor character to convey a large amount of meaning in a short amount of time.

Sir Toby Belch

Sir Toby is Olivia's uncle, and he uses this familial tie to justify staying at her place and making as much of a ruckus as he pleases. Olivia disapproves of his rowdiness, heavy drinking, and late night partying, but generally has other more important things on her mind (like sexy Cesario).

Shakespeare has given this character an aptronym, so that Sir Toby *Belch*'s name sounds as disgusting as he is himself. **He shuns societal expectations, such as those surrounding his noble birth by speaking almost exclusively in prose, being flagrantly drunk all the time and fraternising with mere servants like Maria and Fabian.** With Maria he goes further, flirting with her and also **respecting her intelligence more than any other man in the play respects that of another woman** (except Viola, because she is disguised as a man herself). For example, he entreats her to "tell us, possess us" of her plan rather than continue with his own in Act 2 Scene 3.

Aptronym: a name that is ironically fitting to one's personality or occupation.

Not only does he thus disregard classism and the patriarchy, but he also ignores basic principles of civility in using Sir Andrew for his money, orchestrating his humiliating fight with Cesario, calling him a coward behind his back, and of course lording over the downfall of Malvolio.

Such unabashed bucking of rules and norms, drunken revelry, and causing of mayhem casts Sir Toby as **an embodiment of the traditional 'Twelfth Night' festivities, and thus as a representation of the 'Lord of Misrule.'**

However, Sir Toby also **abandons his apparently egalitarian ideals when it suits him,** using classism to put down Malvolio, and thoughtlessly ordering around Maria in Act 2 Scene 3. Thus, it is evident that **Sir Toby is only out for himself**, seeking to have the most fun as he can, while he can.

His fun does come to an end however, when he **disavows drunkenness, shuns Sir Andrew, and marries Maria in the final Act. Being symbolic of the Lord of Misrule, these actions demonstrate an end to the period of allowed misadventure, and the return to normal societal stringencies.**

Maria

Maria is Olivia's "gentlewoman" – basically a lady in waiting whose job is to keep Olivia company, attend to her needs, and help keep the household running.

As **the only character that is both a member of the lower social classes *and* a woman,** Maria resides in the intersection of two underprivileged groups and as such is an **embodiment of the oppressed.** However, she does not let this define her. **In defiance of societally mandated gender stereotypes of women, she is intelligent and sexually empowered** (see Act 1 Scene 3), and in contravention of the classist narrative **her ability to convincingly impersonate the upper class (by forging a letter from Olivia) reinforces the idea that social rank is performative. Thus, Maria personifies an anti-establishment audacity.**

Audacity: bravery or willingness to take risks.

This rebellious spirit is encouraged and enabled by Sir Toby because it aligns with his devil-may-care philosophy of debauchery and misrule. But what does she see in him? Maria shares witty banter with Sir Toby, showing that he shares her intelligence and sense of humour, and his respect for her (discussed above) despite her lowly position give her an outlet and a partner with which to **fight the status quo, as personified by Malvolio.**

Sir Toby gradually becomes more commanding of her, his last line to her being an instruction to "come by and by to my chamber," and then Maria is never seen in the play again. We later learn that they got married, and so the return to order pushes the oppressed once again out of sight and mind. **Thus in Maria's triumph and fall of independence and agency, Shakespeare charts the triumph and fall of the play's festive and rebellious spirit.**

Sir Andrew Aguecheek

Sir Andrew is supposedly staying at Olivia's house in order to woo her, but he does very little wooing during the play and instead spends most of his time as Sir Toby's drinking buddy.

Like Sir Toby, **Shakespeare has given Sir Andrew an aptronym,** as 'Ague' refers to illnesses involving fever and shivering like malaria. This name is apt because it **reflects Sir Andrew's feebleness of character** (as opposed to physical feebleness in the face of disease), being an idiot and a coward. It also refers literally to the hollowness of his cheeks which is picked on by Sir Toby throughout the text ("Agueface" and "thin-faced knave"), probably making fun of the original actor.

His love of singing, drinking, and dancing helps to **fuel the play's festive atmosphere,** and his gullibility allows Sir Toby to manipulate him out of his money and his dignity (if he ever had any). **Thus, Shakespeare presents Sir Andrew as a character designed to entertain the audience by virtue of schadenfreude.**

Schadenfreude: pleasure derived from the misfortune of others. It's a German word, but in fairly common English usage because it's such a universal experience.

However, he's not just a character to laugh at; believe it or not there is a little more depth of meaning here. In his sword fight with 'Cesario,' Sir Andrew pretends to be full of bravado and swagger, but abandons this pretence as soon as he thinks that Cesario has called his bluff. With this moment **Shakespeare comments on the ambiguity of masculinity, reinforcing the idea that 'manliness' can be faked – just like with Viola's disguise – and so challenges the validity of gender roles.** His impotence also challenges the class system, as it shows that just because you have a noble title like 'Sir' doesn't implicitly make you better than anyone else.

His failure to achieve his goal (Olivia's hand in marriage) by the play's end reflects his failure to uphold societal expectations of men and the bourgeoisie during the **crucible** of misrule. Thus, Shakespeare uses Sir Andrew's character not only to make the audience laugh, but to indict the challenge he embodied to the prejudices of society.

Crucible: a melting pot with very high temperatures (here used figuratively to refer to a very severe trial).

Feste

Feste is a fool, but that's only his job description, not a commentary on his intelligence. On the contrary, he is probably **the wittiest and wisest person in Illyria** (as Viola points out in Act 3 Scene 1, "this fellow is wise enough to play the Fool, / And to do that well craves a kind of wit").

Olivia describes him as "an allowed fool," which means he has permission to do and say whatever he wants to whoever he wants; so long as he's clever and funny he can insult rich, powerful people without fear of punishment. However, unlike with the licensed misrule of the masses during 'Twelfth Night,' Feste's foolery doesn't ultimately serve the establishment.

Indeed, **Feste doesn't really challenge the system so much as exist *outside* of its rules of time** (his unpunished "lateness" to Olivia's court), **place** (moves freely between the upper and lower ranks of both Olivia and Orsino's court, remarking that foolery "walk[s] around the orb like the sun"), **class** (he is witty and learned, yet earns money through begging, and freely associates with people of all classes), **gender** (he shows no 'manly' qualities of strength in fighting, strict logic, or emotional reservedness, and *is not punished* for this like Sir Andrew and Antonio are), **and love** (neither seeking nor being sought by another).

There is also evidence that his detachment is not just from society as it is presented in the play, but also from the play itself. He is eerily good at sizing up other characters, for example noting Orsino's "opal" mind and Viola's suspicious lack of a "beard," and makes multiple meta-textual allusions to the fact that he is in a performance. **This suggests a potential omniscience that extends beyond the boundaries of the play to acknowledge and connect with the audience.**

So, Feste knows he's in a play, he knows the plot of that play, its rules never seem to apply to him, and he's a total genius at wordplay. Remind you of anyone? Yep, I'm looking at you, Shakespeare. It makes sense that **Feste represents the playwright or storyteller, his entire job is to entertain his audience with words and performance.**

The implications of this are that you should **pay close attention to his songs** and anything he says that doesn't seem like simple silliness. **Shakespeare often uses Feste to make comments on the action and themes of the play** which, given that he exists on a different plane to the other characters, present **a level of objectivity that other characters cannot match.**

Olivia

Olivia is a countess of Illyria and, according to popular opinion, the most beautiful woman in existence. That's a big call, but their opinions may have been coloured by the fact that she is also the most eligible bachelorette in the country. The deaths of her father and brother have left her with a **unique level of empowerment,** in charge of the family money and with no man to tell her what to do. In a strongly patriarchal society, most guys seem think this is an issue, and suitors like Orsino, Sir Andrew, and even Malvolio try to take back that power.

But Olivia is more than just beautiful and uniquely rich (for a woman) – we see in her initial interaction with 'Cesario' that **she's smart, sassy, and independent.** She doesn't want to marry someone of a higher social status, because she wants to maintain power within her relationship when she does decide to marry.

From a feminist perspective, Olivia's values and empowerment are admirable. However, Olivia is so preoccupied with her self-imposed seven years of mourning that she cannot use her unique position to engage with and enjoy the world around her. In her own way, **Olivia begins the play just as self-absorbed as Orsino.** That's not to say that she shouldn't grieve her brother's death, but shutting herself away from the world for seven years? She herself admits to being bored when Feste shows up ("for want of other idleness"), and seems happy enough for him to point out that her reaction is a bit excessive. Thus Shakespeare demonstrates that love which cannot be reciprocated by another person is detrimental.

But Viola comes along to steal Olivia's heart and drag her out of her slump. **Olivia's feelings for 'Cesario' demonstrates a few important principles about love.** Her explanation of what exactly she has fallen for – "thy tongue, thy face, thy limbs, actions and spirit" – show that she is infatuated with Cesario as a full person, not merely for his appearance. However appearance is a part of it, and thus it is suggested that androgyny can be attractive. Furthermore, Olivia declares that these qualities "give [Cesario] fivefold **blazon,**" implying that his traits make him as worthy as someone from a noble family. Thus **Shakespeare presents through Olivia the concept that true love (as opposed to purely physical or opportunistic attraction) may disregard, gender, class, and also age** (she describes him as a "youth", implying he is younger than her).

Blazon: a coat of arms denoting one's family

As though her independence, smarts, and attraction to Cesario weren't socially transgressive enough, Olivia takes it a step further. Rather than moping about, merely daydreaming about him, she proactively pursues and proposes to him. At this point, **Olivia couldn't be farther from the traditional Elizabethan notions of the "ideal" woman who is silent, chaste, and obedient.** All of this makes Olivia just as unruly and rebellious in her own way as characters like Sir Toby and Maria, adding to all of the 'misrule' of the play.

In portraying strong, intelligent, independent female characters like Olivia Shakespeare helped abolish one-dimensional stereotypes about women. However, they do all still end up married off. For Olivia this means giving up her independence and wealth to essentially a stranger, as she marries Viola's twin brother Sebastian by mistake. This **ultimately results in the restoration of societal norms of heterosexuality, patriarchy, and class.**

Malvolio

Malvolio is Olivia's steward (i.e. head servant). He's obnoxious and uppity and never misses an opportunity to criticise others, putting down Feste's fooling, Sir Toby's partying, and basically anything even slightly fun. Because of this, **pretty much everyone hates him.** Maria describes him as "a kind of puritan," which was a religious group **known for opposing cross-dressing, theatre, rowdiness and most forms of entertainment.** Although Malvolio is not actually identified as a Puritan, his alignment with them casts him as an easy villain to theatre-going audiences, and an **embodiment of rules and social order. Thus, as he is humiliated by Sir Toby (our 'Lord of Misrule' figure), the social order that he symbolises is likewise turned over to "madness."**

But Sir Toby's fun does end, and **as Malvolio vows to be "revenged on the whole pack of you" it is symbolically implied that social convention will rise again** and punish those who partook of the misrule with too much gusto. Indeed, by the time he makes his threat, that 'return' has already begun.

However, Malvolio is not quite a perfect incarnation of social norms, as he is also a **social climber.** His wish to marry Olivia is not driven by love, but rather by aspirations to wear fancy clothes, boss around the servants, and have the rank to give Sir Toby a good dressing-down. **In a world strictly divided by class, his coveting of Olivia's power goes against what would be considered 'proper'. So, ironically, even as his being locked in darkness and made fun of symbolises the height of misrule's triumph over propriety, it simultaneously punishes his hubris and entrenches the class system.**

Personally, I think the trick that is played on Malvolio went a little too far. In fact **many modern productions and audiences make Malvolio a sympathetic character.** Sure, he's an uptight party-pooper, but locking him in a dark house for days on end, making him question his own sanity, and probably losing him his job seem disproportionate to the crime. It is even compared to bear-baiting by Sir Toby ("we'll have the bear again; and we will fool him [Malvolio/the bear] black and blue"), a sport which is objectively awful and condemned by the lady Olivia. Nevertheless, the audience is encouraged to laugh at Malvolio's humiliation, and usually does. This, then, **implicates us in the maltreatment, and Shakespeare thus forces us to question our own morality.** Is the sheer cruelty of treating a person like a madman worth our entertainment?

Antonio

Antonio is a sea pirate (although he refutes that label) who rescued Sebastian from the Shipwreck that saw Viola washed up on Illyria. After three months at sea, they too arrive on Illyria's shore. During their three months together, alone, on a boat, they developed a very close bond. **Whether they are simply close friends or lovers though (although both could be true) is up for debate,** as it is never made explicate. Either way, their relationship is significant in the way that it dramatises male connection. It is interesting that **neither Antonio nor Sebastian's love for one another is characterised as madness, as so much love within the play is.** It is only when they find themselves in situations where their love (or someone else's love for them, in Sebastian's case) is unrequited that they join the chaos, suggesting that **only unrequited love is wrong, while love that is shared is good.**

Antonio as an individual is **brave, loyal, and good with a sword.** All qualities which lend themselves to the image of the 'ideal' man. However, his **frequent declarations of love for Sebastian rather the, say, simple strong friendship and admiration, does contravene Elizabethan heteronormativity.** And although he respects his place within the class system, offering to be Sebastian's servant when he finds out that Sebastian is of a noble family, he doesn't hold material wealth in too high a regard, giving Sebastian his purse and loving him for his "venerable worth" rather than his money. Thus, **Antonio understands and mostly adheres to societal expectations, but potentially does not agree with them, or at least doesn't hold them in high regard.** Perhaps this is why, in the end, his (possible) lover Sebastian ends up married to Olivia, while he ends up in chains.

Sebastian

Sebastian is **Viola's twin brother,** who is assumed dead until Act 2, and assumes that his sister is dead until Act 5. Although, we don't see much of Sebastian during the play, he is **very significant to its plot and resolution.** On arrival he removes the disguise that he adopted at sea, but ironically then has his identity mistaken for 'Cesario,' and ultimately marries Olivia.

Sebastian is intelligent, skilful in a fight, decisive and action oriented, and a total gentleman to boot. He is also literally a gentleman, being of the same noble birth as Viola, and (unlike other noble characters in the play) **adheres to the decorum that is therefore expected of him,** for example he treats his (lower status) rescuer Antiono with respect yet authority in commanding him not follow when he heads to Orsino's court. Unlike Antonio, Sebastian has plenty of gratitude and amicability towards his boat buddy but never professes to "love" him. Thus, **Sebastian is the perfect model of societal expectations during the play and, accordingly, ends up with the most favourable outcome of any character.**

Fabian

Fabian is a very lowly servant of Olivia. His position has the lowest status in the play. Although there are other low-profile servants, such as Orsino's Curio and Valentine, Fabian's position in Olivia's household is clearly lower than even Maria's (although he does enjoy male privilege) as he does not wait on his master directly, indeed does not even speak with her until the very end of the play. Along with Feste, Fabian is also one of only two characters (excepting Orsino's aforementioned servants and the Priest, who's measly total of eight lines of pure exposition *combined* make them fairly insignificant) whose **judgement is not confused by love.** Thus, as an **objective witness and enabler of the chaos** reaped by Sir Toby and the gang, **Fabian is to some extent a reflection of the audience.**

Priest

The nameless priest shows up in the final Act to confirm that Olivia and 'Cesario' are married, having in fact married Olivia and Sebastian. His arrival signifies the return of the strict rules and morality of religion and matrimony.

Section 5

Key Themes Analysis

Rules and order

The title of *Twelfth Night* refers to a traditional winter festival in which all the rules of social order were inverted, when servants commanded their masters, insults were thrown, and everyone indulged in drinking and crazy, riotous behaviour for a period of licensed misrule. Likewise, the play itself is full of drinking, singing, dancing, and **social transgression against conventions like civility, the class system, heteronormativity, and gender roles.**

None embodies this festive spirit as perfectly as Sir Toby Belch, in his total disregard for what is expected of him as a man, an aristocrat, and a decent human being. In this character, **Shakespeare creates a representation of the traditional 'Lord of Misrule'.**

Antithesis: total opposite.

Shakespeare also **creates Sir Toby's antithesis in Malvolio**, whose strict adherence and enforcement of social convention and alignment with the puritan movement casts him as a **representation of social order** itself. Thus in their clash of personalities, **Shakespeare charts the rise and fall of the carnivalesque licensed misrule.**

At its height, Sir Toby's humiliation of Malvolio becomes undeniably cruel, locking him in darkness and treating him as though he is possessed by the devil. But, like the festival for which the play is named, the madness must come to an end, and Malvolio symbolically vows revenge as the social order reinstates itself.

With this play, Shakespeare thus celebrates the wild spirit of misrule, while also acknowledging the role of rules order in preserving the fine line between fun chaos and cruel anarchy.

Class and society

Many of the characters in *Twelfth Night* are seeking to change their social status in some way. Malvolio wants to marry up, Olivia wants to marry down. Sir Andrew, Sir Toby, and Viola are noble characters that act like the lower classes, and Maria is a servant who impersonates her noble lady in a forged letter. **In this blurring of decorum, Shakespeare challenges the validity of the class system on the basis of the personalities of bourgeois and proletariat characters.**

The ending somewhat dampens this discussion as the status quo of the class system is largely restored, with both Orsino and Olivia marrying the twins (who are within their social station), Malvolio punished for his social ambition, and Sir Andrew punished for his ignoble idiocy.

However, this is not to suggest that the play supports a classist worldview. Although it **sticks the genre conventions of a Shakespearean comedy (in which the world must be thrown into chaos but invariably return to balance and affirm social order)** in order to please his audience which *included aristocrats*, Shakespeare does rebel in having the noble Sir Toby marry the servant Maria. Sure, it happens off-stage and is the *only* thing that doesn't adhere to the classist narrative, but it's one little thorn in proper society's side with which **Shakespeare subtly maintains the play's rebellion against class even into the return to order.**

Gender

Women

Olivia, Maria, and Viola demonstrate that women can be powerful, intelligent, sassy, sexually empowered, proactive *and* still be desirable to men. Through these characters, **Shakespeare makes a strong statement against Elizabethan female stereotypes.** The fact that this is not merely implied, but made explicate in Viola's challenge of Orsino's preconceptions about women being meek and dispassionate in Act 2 Scene 4, suggests that Shakespeare's challenge to male superiority in this play may be didactic.

However, the fact that there are **only three female characters, compared to twelve males,** means that regardless of how well rounded the women are they **cannot possibly represent femininity as fully as the male characters represent masculinity.**

Men

Through the play's male characters, **Shakespeare presents innumerable facets of the male identity.** These include Orsino's poetry and temperamental nature, Sir Andrew's cowardice, Sir Toby's drunkenness, Malvolio's love of rules, Antonio's loyalty, and Sebastian's skill with fighting. With all of these collective contrasting traits and abilities, **Shakespeare suggests that masculinity is subjective, and that men can be anything.**

Other

Some critics argue that the play doesn't stop at exploring binary gender, and that through Viola's disguise the ideas of gender ambiguity and fluidity are examined. I would challenge this, as **although Viola may *appear* androgynous and so challenge the necessity of gender in love** (see the following discussion of the theme of love), **she remains adamant in her self-identification as a female,** constantly referring to herself as a woman in asides to the audience.

However, the fact that everybody else accepts her as a male does **suggest that gender is performed for society rather than defined by your sex.** Similarly, all actors in Shakespeare's era were men, so the same concept of performative gender would have been suggested by the men giving performances of Olivia and Maria.

The ending

As with class and society, in **the final Act the play restores conventional notions of gender** by revealing Viola's disguise and confirming the man/woman duality and power dynamic with heterosexual marriages. ***However*****,** again as with class and society, this is not to suggest that the play supports a sexist or gender normative worldview; although Viola reveals her identity, she remains in her male clothes, and **although Orsino knows she is 'Viola' and has agreed to make her his wife he still calls her 'boy' and 'Cesario.'** Maybe he just needs some time to adjust to the change in his reality, maybe he fell in love with Viola as a boy, or maybe he loves her as both a woman and man. Arguments can be made for all sorts of interpretations, but there's no way to know for sure. And since it is left ambiguous, we are left wondering how and to what extent **the play rebels against socially acceptable assumptions regarding gender for the Elizabethans.**

Disguise and deceit

Every major character in the play deceives at least one other at some point: Viola disguises herself as Cesario, Orsino and Malvolio insincerely claim to love Olivia, Olivia lies to Malvolio to send Viola her ring, Sir Toby and Fabian lie to Sir Andrew and Viola to make them fight, Sir Andrew pretends to be brave in his letter, Maria forges a letter to seem like Olivia wrote it, Sebastian called himself Roderigo, Antonio denies his identity to resist arrest, and Feste disguises himself as 'Sir Topas the Curate' to torture Malvolio. Meta-textually speaking, there is also the fact that every character is in fact an actor 'in disguise.' **Shakespeare thus exposes the universality of deception.**

But in the end, every disguise is dropped and every lie exposed, including the make-believe of the play itself, as Feste acknowledges that the performance and its purpose as entertainment. By drawing back the curtain, the audience is shown how some lies are told for good reason and don't have a negative consequence. For example, Sebastian calls himself Roderigo to disguise his heritage and protect himself from potential kidnap; however, since his intentions were never harmful, there is no falling out between him and Antonio when he comes clean. **Hence, the play considers the idea, contrary to the knee-jerk instinct to condemn deception, that it is the *intention* behind the disguise, not the disguise itself, which has moral implications.**

However, the play also warns that the differences in the perceptions of reality, often caused by deliberate deception, can create a disconnect between people. For example, Maria's deceptive letter to Malvolio places the steward and his lady on very different planes of comprehension such that neither can understand the other's perspective, leading to a **mutual lack of empathy** wherein Malvolio thinks Olivia is cruelly toying with him, Olivia believes he has gone mad, and neither are aware of the reality. **So Shakespeare encourages the audience to consider the differences between perception and reality, and challenges us to acknowledge how our own facades and social identities diverge from our true selves.**

Love

Love is compared throughout the play via simile and metaphor to three main things: music, the ocean, and life/death. The common thread between these images is **transience**, as tides, melodies, and youth come and go and are never the same from one moment to the next. **Love is thus also connoted to be transient.** This is consistent with Olivia's convenient transference of affection from Cesario to Sebastian, and with Orsino's from Olivia to Viola. Only Viola and Antonio are really loyal in their love, almost self-destructively so; they both do what would make their loved one happy (Viola tries to make Olivia fall in love with Orsino, Antonio gives Sebastian his purse) to their own detriment. **Thus, *Twelfth Night's* plot suggests the folly of eternal love.**

Transience: the state or fact of lasting only for a short time.

It equally points out the madness of one-sided love. Consistently, characters that love unrequitedly are described as mad or aligned with the devil. For example, Olivia says that she is as mad as Malvolio for pining for Viola, and when Olivia gives Sebastian love which he does not initially return, he questions his own sanity. The same can be said for the self absorbed narcissism of Orsino, whose love poetry for Olivia is called **heresy.**

Heresy: contrary to religion.

However, **this is not to say that the play presents all love as foolish** – it only critiques love that is misdirected. Neither Antonio nor Sebastian are described mad in their love for one another, and Sir Toby and Maria's relationship only makes them stronger as a united force against authority; it is never criticised or characterised negatively. Thus **love itself, when shared mutually between two people, characterised as a purely positive emotion.**

There is of course a contrast between the **deep passion** professed by everyone in the Orsino/Olivia/Cesario/Viola love triangle, and the simple **banter and familiarity** that Maria and Toby find. **The play also, even as it moves toward an ending of sanctioned heterosexual marriages, examines through homoerotic imagery** (i.e. all that talk of unsheathed swords) **the potential for same-sex desire** between Sebastian/Antonio and Orsino/Cesario. With the evocation of these relationships the play encourages the audience (at least the modern audience) to **consider where the boundaries between male friendship, romance, and lust begin and end.** Indeed, there is the suggestion that **gender may be an irrelevant factor in the consideration of love, given that both male and female characters are attracted to the androgynous Cesario.**

The play doesn't push *all* of the boundaries regarding love though, as all of the relationships are portrayed with exclusively monogamous desire.

Section 6

Structural Feature Analysis

Shakespearean comedy genre

Twelfth Night is a comedy. However, being a Shakespearian comedy means that there are a few more criteria than just being funny. Indeed, not all of Shakespeare's plays included in the 'comedy' category of the First Folio are particularly funny at all. *The Winter's Tale* is a 'comedy', for example, that dramatises violence, anger, and bitter jealously, where characters are murdered by Gods and ripped apart by bears. The main thing that the comedies have in common is that, **after a period of general craziness, they all end in marriage** (or at least betrothal).

Much of the actual **comedy often comes from the confusion of lovers, usually arising from unlikely misunderstandings and intentional deceptions.** Shakespeare's comedies therefore **rely on substantial amounts of dramatic irony,** whereby the audience knows things that the bewildered lovers do not, until the institution of marriage comes along to restore convention, representing happiness and the promise of children to continue the family name.

Shakespeare also often makes use of disguise in his comedies, most often disguising women as young men. For example, the play *As You Like It* involves a man practising how to woo his beloved with a young man, who is in fact his beloved in disguise!

While most comedies by other playwrights contemporary to Shakespeare took place in England during the Elizabethan period, Shakespeare himself uniquely **chose the settings for his comedies to be in foreign or fictional locations and during an undisclosed, timeless era** (only one was set in England, *The Merry Wives of Windsor*). For example, the imaginary magical wood outside Athens in *A Midsummer Night's Dream* or the Forest of Arden in *As You Like It,* or our very own Illyria in *Twelfth Night.*

It was also typical of Shakespeare to include **moments of tragedy** in his comedies (as well as moments of comedy in his tragedies), which could include Viola, Olivia, and Sebastian's grief for dead siblings, or the sorrow of Sir Andrew losing his only friend.

Paragon: the epitome, or perfect example of something.

Twelfth Night adheres to all of these genre conventions perfectly, making it the **paragon** of the Shakespearean comedy.

Act/scene breakdown

In *Twelfth Night*, Shakespeare **varies the tone and length of scenes** drastically and often **juxtaposes contrasting features of consecutive scenes,** such as jumping from the lazily love-lorn Orsino's music-filled castle suddenly onto the beach where Viola grieves for her dead brother. **This scattered chronology reflects the madness of the play itself.** Thus, the final Act when order is restored is in itself one mammoth scene, indicating the **initiation of stability.**

There are, however, some structural conventions adhered to throughout the play. **Scenes spoken in verse often signify their end with a rhyming couplet.** More macrocosmically, the **rhyming couplet also closes the first and fourth Acts, bookending the period of most intense misrule.**

The scene order can also be analysed in terms of when characters are introduced. **Ostensibly, Viola is the protagonist** of *Twelfth* Night, given that it is her actions that spark much of the action (and confusion). She even indirectly enables the whole Malvolio debacle by distracting Olivia from her duties as head of her estate. **However the first scene is not given to Viola, it is given to Orsino** to make long self-absorbed monologues about passion and love. Structurally, the play therefore prioritises the rich guy over every other character, and thus **establishes that Illyria is a classist patriarchy.** Another technique Shakespeare uses is reputation. **Olivia doesn't appear onstage until after she has been described** by Orsino, the Sea Captain, Sir Toby, Maria, and Sir Andrew. Thus the audience is encouraged to desire her by virtue of her reputation of being desired, and to pity her based on second-hand accounts of her grief, before we have a chance to judge her for ourselves. In this way **Shakespeare builds up our anticipation of her character to make it all the more powerful when she does appear.**

Language

Shakespeare's entire craft as a poet and playwright was built around words and language. Unlike in a book, where the majority of the story can be told through the author's own narrative voice, **in a play the author must create different, unique 'voices' for each character** with their specific turns of phrase and grammatical **idiosyncrasies**. For example, Sir Toby's tendency to make up nonsensical phrases like "taste your legs" and run his words together as in "h'as hurt me, and there's th'end on't" is quite unlike Orsino's poetical and elevated vocabulary.

Idiosyncrasy: behaviour, thought, or rhythm of speech that is unique to an individual.

A large part of a character's voice is whether they speak in **verse or prose.** Verse often indicates education, so generally upper classes speak in verse, lower classes in prose. However, if a member of the upper classes is drunk, stupid, or speaking with less pretension, they are more likely to speak in prose, like Sir Toby and Sir Andrew. Likewise, when moved to great emotion a member of the lower classes may speak in verse.

There is an important distinction to make between verse and poetry. Shakespeare wrote over 150 poems separate from his plays, 154 of which were sonnets, so he knows how to write a good love poem! It's no accident then that **Orsino's declarations of love to Olivia are *not* good love poems.** Being riddled with clichéd images comparing beauty to flowers and nature, **Shakespeare mocks this popular formula as unoriginal** through Olivia's declaration that she has already "read" the poems of Orsino's heart, and she **exposes how formulaic poetry can lose credibility** in her rebuff that "poetical" assertions are more "like[ly] to be feigned," and **parodies poems that systematically compare female features to nature**; "item, two lips indifferent red; item, two grey eyes, with lids to them."

However, Shakespeare **also displays the power of poetry when composed sincerely,** such as how Olivia falls in love with 'Cesario' when Viola abandons parroting Orsino's forced poem in favour of her own spontaneous "willow cabin" fantasy.

Just as the author demonstrates the shortcomings of poetry, he also **uses language to expose how words can be "corrupted" by figures like Feste, how language can lie even as is reveals truths and wisdom.**

Symbolism

Any object or character in *Twelfth Night* could be imbued with symbolism given you have a plausible argument and textual evidence for it.

In my opinion, the most symbolic single object of the play is **the ring that Olivia sends in chase of Viola.** On the surface, it is a symbol of Olivia's wealth, and also of marriage. Thus, **In rejecting it, Viola rejects Olivia's love and wealth.** More abstractly, the ring is (geometrically speaking) a physical manifestation of cycles without beginning or ending, thus **symbolising the timelessness of the play, and the cycles of rule and misrule, of life and death, of disguise and reveal,** that have perpetuated (as Feste notes) since "a great while ago [when] the Earth begun." In this way it is similar to the ocean motif, whose endless waves are linked to love and life in its all-encompassing nature.

Many other trinkets are given away as love gifts; a piece of jewellery with Olivia's miniature portrait, a pearl, and Orsino sends her a jewel as well. **The thoughtless frequency with which these tokens are dispensed demonstrate Olivia and Orsino's carelessness with the love and wealth which they symbolise. By contrast, Malvolio's reaction to the mere thought of "some rich jewel" shows how much he covets wealth.**

While jewels seem to have the same meaning for everyone, **some objects can have different significance depending on one's perspective.** Payment, for example, is given by Viola to anyone who can make her smile (such as the Sea Captain and Feste), and so represents her generosity and the value placed on happiness. By contrast, Sir Andrew flagrantly wastes his money so that for him is becomes evidence to his foolishness.

Characters are also symbolic. As discussed on pages 39 and 43, Sir Toby becomes a symbol for misrule, and Malvolio a symbol for order, and so through their interactions, Shakespeare can comment on the state of affairs in Illyria at any point in the plot. Likewise, Maria symbolises oppression, Orsino symbolises privilege, Fabian symbolises the audience, and Feste symbolises the playwright himself.

Metatheatricality

A number of times in *Twelfth Night*, **characters make references to the fact that they are in a play.** This draws attention to the unreality and theatricality of the performance. Such a distancing tactic shatters the illusion of immersion, **forcing us to consciously consider the play and its meanings beyond simple entertainment.** For example, from a meta-textual perspective, Feste's triumph over Malvolio could represent the triumph of theatre over puritanism, a kind of catharsis for Shakespeare and an easy villain for the theatre-loving audience.

Reminding the audience that they are watching a play also justifies the farcical elements as entertainment rather than reality; instead of allowing the ridiculousness of the action to distance the audience, **the play parodies itself to unite the performers and the audience in the ridicule of the characters.**

Some characters go further than unwittingly reminding the audience of the performance, and actually imply that they *themselves* are **aware of being inside a play.** In Feste's case, the frequency and specificity of such statements suggests a **potential omniscience** that extends beyond the boundaries of the play to acknowledge and connect with the audience. The implications of this are that **Shakespeare often uses Feste to make comments on the action and themes of the play with a level of objectivity that other characters cannot match.**

Section 7

Quote Bank

Rules and order

Quote	Character	Act/Scene
"My lady takes great exception to your ill hours... you must confine yourself within the modest limits of order."	Maria	Act 1 Scene 3
"My lady will hang thee for thy absence."	Maria	Act 1 Scene 5
"What think you of this fool, Malvolio? Doth he not mend?"	Olivia	Act 1 Scene 5
"I marvel your lady takes delight in such a barren rascal."	Malvolio	Act 1 Scene 5
"There is no slander in an allowed fool though he do nothing but rail; nor no railing in a known discreet man though he do nothing but reprove."	Olivia	Act 1 Scene 5
"And the fool shall look to the madman"	Feste	Act 1 Scene 5
"O time, thou must untangle this, not I; It is too hard a knot for me t'untie."	Viola	Act 2 Scene 2
"To be up after midnight and go to bed then is early; so that to go to bed after midnight is to go to bed betimes."	Sir Toby	Act 2 Scene 2
"My masters, are you mad?... Is there no respect of place, persons, nor time in you?"	Malvolio	Act 2 Scene 3
"Dost thou think that because thou art virtuous there shall be no more cakes and ale?"	Sir Toby	Act 2 Scene 3
"Mistress Mary, if you prized my lady's favour at anything more than contempt, you would not give means for this uncivil rule"	Malvolio	Act 2 Scene 3
"The devil a puritan that [Malvolio] is... a time-pleaser, an affectioned ass, that cons state without book... [and thinks] that all that look on him love him."	Maria	Act 2 Scene 3

"Pleasure will be paid, one time or another."	Feste	Act 2 Scene 4
"Be opposite with a kinsman, surly with servants; let thy tongue tang arguments of state; put thyself into the trick of singularity"	Malvolio	Act 2 Scene 5
"Words are grown so false, I am loath to prove reason with them."	Feste	Act 3 Scene 1
"Foolery, sir, does walk about the orb like the sun, it shines every where."	Feste	Act 3 Scene 1
"This fellow is wise enough to play the fool"	Viola	Act 3 Scene 1
"Why, this is very midsummer madness."	Olivia	Act 3 Scene 4
"If this were played upon a stage now, I could condemn it as an improbable fiction."	Fabian	Act 3 Scene 4
"Why, we shall make him mad indeed."	Fabian	Act 3 Scene 4
"There's something in me that reproves my fault; But such a headstrong potent fault it is, That it but mocks reproof."	Olivia	Act 3 Scene 4
"Are all the people mad?"	Sebastian	Act 4 Scene 1
"Never was man thus wronged: good Sir Topas, do not think I am mad: they have laid me here in hideous darkness."	Malvolio	Act 4 Scene 2
"Now go with me and with this holy man... And underneath that consecrated roof, / Plight me the full assurance of your faith"	Olivia	Act 4 Scene 3
"A contract of eternal bond of love"	Priest	Act 5 Scene 1
"I hate a drunken rogue... an ass-head, and a coxcomb, and a knave, a thin-faced knave, a gull"	Sir Toby	Act 5 Scene 1
"So it comes, lady, you have been mistook. But nature to her bias drew in that. You would have been contracted to a maid"	Sebastian	Act 5 Scene 1
"Your master quits you; and for your service done him, / So much against the mettle of your sex, / So far below your soft and tender breeding... you shall from this time be / Your mater's mistress."	Orsino	Act 5 Scene 1

"Maria writ / The letter... In recompense whereof [Sir Toby] hath married her"	Fabian	Act 5 Scene 1
"And thus the whirligig of time brings in his revenges."	Feste	Act 5 Scene 1
"I'll be revenged on the whole pack of you!"	Malvolio	Act 5 Scene 1
"A great while ago the world begun, / With hey, ho, the wind and the rain, / But that's all one, our play is done, / And we'll strive to please you every day."	Feste	Act 5 Scene 1

Class and society

Quote	Character	Act/Scene
"What great ones do, the less will prattle of"	Sea Captain	Act 1 Scene 2
"O that I served that lady... Till I had made mine own occasion mellow / What my estate is!"	Viola	Act 1 Scene 2
"I'll pay thee bounteously"	Viola	Act 1 Scene 2
"[Sir Andrew] has three thousand ducats a year."	Sir Toby	Act 1 Scene 3
"Ay, but... [Sir Andrew is] a very fool and a prodigal."	Maria	Act 1 Scene 3
"[Olivia will] not match above her degree, neither in estate, years, nor wit."	Sir Toby	Act 1 Scene 3
"[Orsino is] virtuous... noble, / Of great estate, of fresh and stainless youth... free, learned, and valiant... A gracious person. But yet I cannot love him."	Olivia	Act 1 Scene 5
"[My parentage is] Above my fortunes, yet my state is well: I am a gentleman."	Viola	Act 1 Scene 5
"I am no fee'd post, lady; keep your purse; My master, not myself lacks recompense."	Viola	Act 1 Scene 5
"If you will not murder me for my love, let me be your servant."	Antonio	Act 2 Scene 1
"Tis not the first time I have constrained one to call me knave."	Sir Andrew	Act 2 Scene 3

"My masters, are you mad?... Have you no wit, manners, nor honesty but to gabble like tinkers at this time of night?"	Malvolio	Act 2 Scene 3
"Art [thou, Malvolio] any more than a steward?"	Sir Toby	Act 2 Scene 3
"I can write very like my lady"	Maria	Act 2 Scene 3
"[Orsino's] mind is a very opal."	Feste	Act 2 Scene 4
"My love, more noble than the world, Prizes not quantity of dirty lands"	Orsino	Act 2 Scene 4
"To be Count Malvolio!"	Malvolio	Act 2 Scene 5
"Some are born great, some achieve greatness, and some have greatness thrust upon 'em."	Malvolio	Act 2 Scene 5
"So thou mayst say, the king lies by a beggar, if a beggar dwell near him; or, the church stands by thy tabour, if thy tabour stand by the church."	Viola	Act 3 Scene 1
"Why appear you with this ridiculous boldness before my lady?"	Maria	Act 3 Scene 4
"Or else the lady's mad; yet, if 'twere so, /She could not sway her house, command her followers, / Take and give back affairs and their dispatch / With such a smooth, discreet and stable bearing / As I perceive she does"	Sebastian	Act 4 Scene 4
"We will our celebration keep / According to my birth."	Olivia	Act 4 Scene 3
"Be that thou know't thou art, and then thou art / As great as that thou fear'st."	Olivia	Act 5 Scene 1
"Think of me as you please. I leave my duty a little unthought of and speak out of my injury."	Fabian	Act 5 Scene 1
"Your master quits you; and for your service done him... So far below your soft and tender breeding... you shall from this time be / Your master's mistress."	Orsino	Act 5 Scene 1

Gender

Quote	Character	Act/Scene
"A virtuous maid, the daughter of a count / That died... her brother... also died; for whose dear love / (They say) she hath abjured the sight / And company of men."	Sea Captain	Act 1 Scene 2
" I pray you bring your hand to h'buttery-bar and let it drink... It's dry, sir."	Maria	Act 1 Scene 3
"I hope to see a huswife take thee between her legs"	Sir Toby	Act 1 Scene 3
"Dear lad... they shall yet belie thy happy years / That say thou art a man: Diana's lip / Is not more smooth and rubious; thy small pipe / Is as the maiden's organ... And all is semblative of a woman's part."	Orsino	Act 1 Scene 4
"Not yet old enough for a man, nor young enough for a boy... One would think his mother's milk were scarce out of him."	Malvolio	Act 1 Scene 5
"'Tis nature truly blent, whose red and white / Nature's own sweet and cunning hand laid on. / Lady, you are the cruellest she alive, / If you will lead these graces to the grave... You are too proud"	Viola	Act 1 Scene 5
"I cannot love him."	Olivia	Act 1 Scene 5
"I am yet so near the manners of my mother that, upon the least occasion more, mine eyes will tell tales of me."	Sebastian	Act 2 Scene 1
"How easy is it for the proper false / In women's waxen hearts to set their forms! / Alas, our frailty is the cause... What thriftless sighs shall pour Olivia breath?"	Viola	Act 2 Scene 2
"Good night, Penthesilea" *(Sir Toby),* "Before me, she's a good wench"	Sir Andrew	Act 2 Scene 3

"Let still the woman take / An elder than herself: so wears she to him, / So sways she level in her husband's heart: / For, boy, however we do praise ourselves, / Our fancies are more giddy and unfirm, / More longing, wavering, sooner lost and worn, Than women's are."	Orsino	Act 2 Scene 4
"Women are as roses, whose fair flower / Being once display'd, doth fall that very hour."	Orsino	Act 2 Scene 4
"And so they [women] are: alas, that they are so; / To die, even when they to perfection grow!"	Viola	Act 2 Scene 4
"'Tis that miracle and queen of gems / That nature pranks [Olivia] in attracts my soul."	Orsino	Act 2 Scene 4
"There is no woman's sides / Can bide the beating of so strong a passion / As love doth give my heart; no woman's heart / So big, to hold so much; they lack retention... make no compare / Between that love a woman can bear me / And that I owe Olivia."	Orsino	Act 2 Scene 4
"In faith, [women] are as true of heart as [men]... [I know a woman who] never told her love... She sat like patience on a monument, / Smiling at grief. Was not this love indeed? / We men may say more, swear more: but indeed / Our shows are more than will; for still we prove / Much in our vows, but little in our love."	Viola	Act 2 Scene 4
"I could marry this wench [Maria] for this device... Wilt thou set thy foot o' my neck?... Shall I play my freedom at tray-trip, and become thy bond-slave?... [I would follow thou] To the gates of Tartar, thou most excellent devil of wit!"	Sir Toby	Act 2 Scene 5
"The Lady Olivia has no folly: she will keep no fool, sir, till she be married; and fools are as like husbands as pilchards are to herrings; the husband's the bigger"	Feste	Act 3 Scene 1
"O, what a deal of scorn looks beautiful / In the contempt and anger of his lip!"	Olivia	Act 3 Scene 1

"I have one heart, one bosom and one truth, / And that no woman has; nor never none / Shall mistress be of it, save I alone."	Viola	Act 3 Scene 1
"As thou drawest swear horrible; for it comes to pass oft that a terrible oath, with a swaggering accent sharply twanged off, gives manhood more approbation than ever proof itself would have earned him."	Sir Toby	Act 3 Scene 4
"My picture; Refuse it not; it hath no tongue to vex you"	Olivia	Act 3 Scene 4
"A little thing would make me tell them how much I lack of a man"	Viola	Act 3 Scene 4
"My masculine usurped attire... my maiden weeds"	Viola	Act 5 Scene 1
"Your master quits you; and for your service done him, / so much against the mettle of your sex... you shall from this time be / Your master's mistress."	Orsino	Act 5 Scene 1

Disguise and deceit

Quote	Character	Act/Scene
"nature with a beauteous wall / Doth oft close in pollution"	Viola	Act 1 Scene 2
"Conceal me what I am... What else may hap, to time I will commit"	Viola	Act 1 Scene 2
"I'll do my best / To woo your lady. Yet a bagful strife! Whoe'er I woo, myself would be his wife."	Viola	Act 1 Scene 4
"Speak to me; I shall answer for her [the honourable lady of the house]"	Olivia	Act 1 Scene 5
"by the very fangs of malice, I swear, I am not that I play. Are you the lady of the house?"	Viola	Act 1 Scene 5
"'tis poetical" *(Viola),* "It is the more like to be feigned"	Olivia	Act 1 Scene 5

"Have you any commission from your lord to negotiate with my face? You are now out of your text, but we will draw the curtain and show you the picture."	Olivia	Act 1 Scene 5
"I see you what you are. You are too proud; / But if you were the devil you are fair!"	Viola	Act 1 Scene 5
"I perceive in you so excellent a touch of modesty that you will not extort from me what I am willing to keep in. Therefore it charges me in manners the rather to express myself. You must know of me then, Antonio, my name is Sebastian (which I called Roderigo)"	Sebastian	Act 2 Scene 1
"I left no ring with her: what means this lady? / Fortune forbid my outside have not charmed her!... I am the man... Poor lady, she were better love a dream."	Viola	Act 2 Scene 2
"Disguise, I see thou art a wickedness"	Viola	Act 2 Scene 2
"If I do not gull [Malvolio] into a ayword, and make him a common recreation, do not think I have wit enough to lie straight in my bed."	Maria	Act 2 Scene 3
"I am all the daughters of my father's house, And all the brothers too"	Viola	Act 2 Scene 4
"[Olivia's] very phrases! By your leave, wax. Soft! and the impressure her Lucrece, with which she uses to seal: 'tis my lady."	Malvolio	Act 2 Scene 5
"I do not now fool myself, to let imagination jade me; for every reason excites to this, that my lady loves me."	Malvolio	Act 2 Scene 5
"I am not what I am"	Viola	Act 3 Scene 1
"O how vile an idol proves this god! // Thou hast, Sebastian, done good feature shame. // In nature there's no blemish but the mind; //None can be call'd deform'd but the unkind:"	Antonio	Act 3 Scene 4
"Nothing that is so is so."	Feste	Act 4 Scene 1

"Nay, I prithee, put on this gown and this beard; make him believe thou art Sir Topas the curate" *(Maria)* "I would I were the first that ever dissembled in such a gown."	Feste	Act 4 Scene 2
"That that is, is"	Feste	Act 4 Scene 2
"This is the air; that is the glorious sun, / This pearl she gave me, I do feel't and see't, / And though 'tis wonder that enwraps me thus, / Yet 'tis not madness... I am ready to distrust mine eyes / And wrangle with my reason... there's something in't / That is deceiveable."	Sebastian	Act 4 Scene 3
"O thou dissembling cub! what wilt thou be / When time hath sow'd a grizzle on thy case? / Or will not else thy craft so quickly grow, / That thine own trip shall be thine overthrow?"	Orsino	Act 5 Scene 1
"One face, one voice, one habit, and two persons, A natural perspective, that is and is not!"	Orsino	Act 5 Scene 1
"How have you made division of yourself? / An apple, cleft in two, is not more twin / Than these two creatures. Which is Sebastian?"	Antonio	Act 5 Scene 1
"I am Viola, which to confirm, / I'll bring you to a captain in this town... by whose gentle help I was preserved"	Viola	Act 5 Scene 1

Love

Quote	Character	Act/Scene
"If music be the food of love, play on, / Give me excess of it that, surfeiting, / The appetite may sicken and so die."	Orsino	Act 1 Scene 1
"Enough, no more, / 'Tis not so sweet now as it was before."	Orsino	Act 1 Scene 1
"O spirit of love... as the sea, naught enters there / Of what validity and pitch so e'er, / But falls into abatement and low price"	Orsino	Act 1 Scene 1

"So full of shapes is fancy / That it alone is high fantastical."	Orsino	Act 1 Scene 1
"How will she love, when the rich golden shaft / Hath killed the flock of all affections else... [when] These sovereign thrones are all supplied and filled / Her sweet perfections with one selfsame king!"	Orsino	Act 1 Scene 1
"Thou know't no less than all: I have unclasped / To thee the book even of my secret soul."	Orsino	Act 1 Scene 4
"If Sir Toby would leave drinking, thou wert as witty a piece of Eve's flesh as any in Illyria."	Feste	Act 1 Scene 5
"In [Orsino's] bosom?... I have read it. It is heresy."	Olivia	Act 1 Scene 5
"[Orsino is] virtuous... noble, / Of great estate, of fresh and stainless youth... free, learned, and valiant... A gracious person. But yet I cannot love him."	Olivia	Act 1 Scene 5
"Thy tongue, thy face, thy limbs, actions, and spirit / Do give thee five-fold blazon... Even so quickly may one catch the plague? / Methinks I feel this youth's perfections"	Olivia	Act 1 Scene 5
"She is drowned already, sir, with salt water, though I seem to drown her remembrance again with more."	Sebastian	Act 2 Scene 1
"I have many enemies in Orsino's court... [But] I do adore [Sebastian] so / That danger shall seem sport, and I will go."	Antonio	Act 2 Scene 1
"Would you have a love song or a song of good life?"	Feste	Act 2 Scene 3
"Journeys end in lovers meeting... What is love? 'Tis not hereafter... What's to come is still unsure... come and kiss me, sweet and twenty; / Youth's a stuff will not endure."	Feste	Act 2 Scene 3
"If ever thou shalt love, / In the sweet pangs of it, remember me: / For such as I am, all true lovers are, / Unstaid and skittish in all motions else, / Save in the constant image of the creature / That is beloved."	Orsino	Act 2 Scene 4

"I pity you" *(Viola)*, "That's a degree to love." *(Olivia)*, "No... very oft we pity enemies."	Viola	Act 3 Scene 1
"Love sought is good, but given unsought better."	Olivia	Act 3 Scene 1
"My desire, / More sharp than filed steel, did spur me forth"	Antonio	Act 3 Scene 3
"How shall I feast him? what bestow of him? // For youth is bought more oft than begg'd or borrow'd."	Olivia	Act 3 Scene 3
"Put up your sword. If this young gentleman / Have done offence, I take the fault on me: / If you offend him, I for him defy you... [I am] One, sir, that for his love dares yet do more / Than you have heard him brag to you he will."	Antonio	Act 3 Scene 4
"A witchcraft drew me hither. / That most ingrateful boy there by your side... His life I gave him and did thereto add / My love, without retention or restraint, / All his in dedication; for his sake / Did I expose myself, pure for his love... Where being apprehended, his false cunning... Taught him to face me out of his acquaintance / And grew a twenty years removed thing"	Antonio	Act 5 Scene 1
"You uncivil lady, To whose ingrate and unauspicious altars / My soul the faithfull'st off'rings have breathed out / That e'er devotion tendered!"	Orsino	Act 5 Scene 1
"I'll sacrifice the lamb that I do love [Cesario] // To spite a raven's heart within a dove."	Orsino	Act 5 Scene 1
"And I, most jocund, apt and willingly, / To do you rest, a thousand deaths would die... After him I love / More than I love these eyes, more than my life"	Viola	Act 5 Scene 1
"Were you a woman – as the rest goes even – / I should my tears let fall upon your cheek, / And say 'Thrice-welcome, drowned Viola.'"	Sebastian	Act 5 Scene 1
"Cesario, come – / For so you shall be, while you are a man, / But when in other habits you are seen, / Orsino's mistress and his fancy's queen."	Orsino	Act 5 Scene 1

Section 8

Sample Essays

Essay One

QUESTION: *Twelfth Night* exploits the fact that the audience cannot believe their own perceptions. Discuss.

ESSAY	COMMENTS
INTRODUCTION In *Twelfth Night,* William Shakespeare exploits the inherent contradictions of his audiences perceptions regarding gender for comic effect.[1] Via the characters and themes explored, the playwright juxtaposes the idealistic fantasies of both the roles and personalities that men and women occupy against reality. In so doing, a balance between the socially acceptable and the distasteful aspects of identity – as defined by gender – is sought in a manner that maybe considered feminist. **PARAGRAPH 1** Shakespeare constructs Olivia as an embodiment of the male perception of female perfection.[2] Orsino idolises "her sweet perfections" and spends almost the entire play pursuing her "love" through various "embass[ies]" while wallowing in the "melancholy" of his "burning passions." Likewise, Sir Andrew is so desperate for Olivia's love that he allows himself to be convinced to"stay a month longer" at the mere suggestion of "her favour" by the manipulative Sir Toby.	1. If you're great at feminist analysis, Marxist analysis, structural analysis, or whatever your secret skill is, then use that to your advantage by knowing how to mould your ideas to suit the essay prompt. Here, the key words in the prompt are 'exploits' and 'perceptions'. In addressing the prompt, you get to define both. Ask yourself what is the audience perceiving? How is Shakespeare manipulating or making use of that? 2. The first paragraph links back directly to the prompt by using one of the key words, 'perception.'

As these characters express their emotions prior to Olivia's own appearance in the play, the audience is encouraged to"desire" her by her reputation of being desired. When her character does materialise, even more traditionally feminine qualities that are stereotypically attractive to men are revealed; she is "the picture" of beauty, reclusive and thus a worth "hart" to "hunt" (the former of being a pun on the word 'heart', thus denoting her love as a prize to be caught and subjugated),[3] and in her infatuation with Cesario reveals a level of impulsive emotional immaturity by "send[ing her] ring" after an pleading with him to "Stay!". This childish dependency cast Olivia, despite her independence and wealth, as an archetypal damsel in distress.[4] Her character is thus designed to be appealing to the testosterone driven urge to not only rescue, but dominate all aspects of a woman's life at the expense of "all affections else." However, this character's pathetic[5] nature, grateful even for "pity" as "a degree to love," is clearly revealed as little more than cliched fantasy when comparing with the more realistic female characters.[6] Shakespeare thus shows his heterosexual male audience members what they may want to see in woman, but utilises their own understanding – subconscious or otherwise – of this image's fallacies to expand the definition of desirability.	3. Occasional 'deep dives' into the metalanguage of a single line or even a single word, where relevant and logical, adds depth to a discussion. 4. Many stories are built around a series of 'archetypes' – sort of stock characters and scenarios that have been around forever. Think fairytale tropes. Identifying where and how a text utilises these archetypes shows an engagement with the wider literary world. 5. This was actually a mistake that I made and my teacher pointed out to me. I wanted to include it to show you what being too judgemental looks like. Remember that your role is to analyse the text, not say whether you like it, or whether you think that its characters are right or wrong. So don't do what I did and call Olivia 'pathetic'! Maintain neutral language and just point out what their actions imply within the context of the play. 6. In the last essay I used the same textual evidence to argue that Olivia is a kick-ass rebel against the patriarchy and the class system! This goes to show that you can argue whatever you want in an essay. You can pick the points that make the most sense to you or will be most useful to your discussion.

PARAGRAPH 2

Shakespeare presents Viola and Maria's fully rounded characters as an antidote to Olivia's shallow depiction. Viola's presentation of herself as the male servant "Cesario" for the majority of the play creates an image of masculinity that serves to the female audience the same role as Olivia's character to the male audience. Cesario is a 'man' whose qualities of "sensitiv[ity]" and willingness to "serve" without desire to subjugate woman (in contrast to Malvolio who, even as a servant and prior to receiving Maria's misleading "letter," fantasises about wedding Olivia to become "Count Malvolio"),[7] appeals is generally to the heterosexual woman. Ironically, this shallow persona provides, of itself, evidence to the complexities of its owner. It demonstrates Viola's adaptability to her environment, gives opportunities for her to display her "wit," and also – crucially – reveals her imperfections as a human being when she realises that the consequent love triangle is "too great a know for me t'untie."[8] This realistic inclusion of both connotatively positive and negative traits is also present in Maria. This character, by her dual role as "gentlewoman" to Olivia and general housekeeper, proves herself to be a highly capable individual. That she is also able to match wits with Feste in the making of "dry jest[s]" also demonstrates her intelligence, and her association with Sir Toby renders her down to earth and unpretentious. However, she uses her intelligence to play an undeniably cruel "trick" on Malvolio. Regardless of one's opinion on whether he deserves it – being "sick of self-love" – Maria procures Malvolio's "suffering," and therefore maybe equally described with negative traits such as vengeful and merciless.

7. If a phrase is getting way too long but you really don't want to break the points you are making into separate sentences, it's okay to occasionally use brackets like this.

8. Rather than just using a quote to explain an external point about a theme, this sentence explains the quote's subtextual implications for the character that said it. Human beings aren't villains or heroes, we all have flaws and strengths. Any character that doesn't is called 'one-dimensional.'

Despite these character flaws which form the crux of the play's comedic rapture, by the denouement Sir Toby "hath married" Maria, and Orsino has accepted Viola as his "queen." Thus it is demonstrated that women of all standings and personalities are worthy of love, even from "above [their] station."[9] However, there remains an unbalanced between Shakespeare's depiction, and therefore the audience's perspective, of men and women characters.

PARAGRAPH 3

Although in his is characterisation of Viola and Maria Shakespeare rounds out the perception of femininity, this is nothing in comparison to his exploration of manliness. In the play's male characters, innumerable facets of the male identity are presented. These include Orsino's "nobility" yet "opal mind" – opal being a stone whose colour changes with the light, symbolic of Orsino's fickle temperament that having achieved something finds it "not so sweet now as... before" – Sir Andrew's "coward[ace]," Sir Toby's "drunkenness," Malvolio's love of "rules," Antonio's loyal "friendship," and Sebastian's skill with fighting, all add to this image of contrasting traits that collectively suggest the infinite potential of man. This causes the extent of the female personae, analysed previously, to pale by comparison, as there are only three women in the entire play. Thus, irrespective of their characterisation as individuals, they cannot represent the female condition as fully as the male characters do masculinity.[10]

9. Once again, this essay uses the same evidence – in this case marriage – to make the opposite point to the last essay. There is no single correct answer, so write whatever makes the most sense to you.

10. This is one of those points that you can memorise and adapt for any essay regarding gender. It is such a big gap that it shouldn't be ignored, and once again it shows engagement beyond just the dialogue, demonstrating your ability to think critically and creatively.

The feminist critic may perceive this as a reflection of either Shakespeare's own bias as a male, the patriarchal nature of the 16th century, or both. However it is highly unlikely that the playwright crafted *Twelfth Night* with feminism in mind,[11] and thus the piece cannot be taken as a comment on gender specifically. Rather, is with the sheer variety of characters that Shakespeare manipulates the audiences perceptions in regards to gender, as much as the characters themselves are manipulated in this narrative of abundant "disguise" and "revelry."

CONCLUSION

In William Shakespeare's comedy *Twelfth Night,* the audience's beliefs regarding gender are challenged in scenarios of such "improbable fiction" that the poet can only have designed them to evoke laughter. Yet, in doing so he has contributed to the destruction of one-dimensional feminine archetypes and thus maybe considered somewhat feminist. While certainly not a 'feminist text' in the sense that it neither portrays nor intended to portray gender equality – indeed, it still ends with all of the female characters losing their independence through marriage – it does prompt the audience to question assumptions and doubt perceptions of gender. Feminist critical lens may thus be applied in acceptance of the Bard's invitation to make of this play 'What You Will.'[12]

11. This is important to note – don't call Shakespeare a feminist or a Marxist, or for that matter a cheese enthusiast! We don't know his opinions, we only know our own interpretations of the implications of his play.

12. For me, a good essay needs to end on what I call a 'boom statement' – a really impactful final note that serves as an impressive, lasting impression on your assessor. This is a great one for *Twelfth Night* that works with almost any essay (with a little adaption).

Essay Two

QUESTION: Shakespeare's romantic comedy *Twelfth Night* is about the ambiguity of socially constructed gender roles. Discuss.

ESSAY	**COMMENTS**
INTRODUCTION Shakespeare's play *Twelfth Night,* through its depiction of femininity and masculinity, presents unique perspectives[1] on the contribution of socially constructed gender roles to the formation and performance of individual identity.[2] By applying a feminist lens,[3] the play's exploration of the restrictive societal definitions of 'male' and 'female' and how these definitions may be stretched or transcended, becomes evident. However, this entertainment of gender ambiguity does not render the text implicitly feminist. Rather, Shakespeare's play must be considered holistically and in context of the Elizabethan era and audience for which it was written, complimentarily to close analysis of language and character, in order to determine what comment *Twelfth Night* ultimately passes on gender.[4]	1. When an essay prompt ends with the word 'discuss', you should address the evidence for as many sides of the argument as you can before reaching a nuanced conclusion. You never have to agree with the statement presented, so feel free to play devil's advocate! 2. In the very first sentence of an introduction, you should include the name of the text, the full name of the author (after that, just their last name is fine), and directly address your spin on the essay prompt. This last part doesn't mean to restate the prompt itself, but rather to incorporate the key words from the prompt and explain your unique take on it. Here, the key words were 'socially constructed gender roles', and 'ambiguity'. I have made it clear that I will be exploring how these roles affect men and women characters. 3. This is an explicit reference to the interpretive perspective that will be used throughout this essay. 4. Swap the last word of this sentence for any theme or significant idea: 'love', 'disguise and deceit', 'rules and order', 'pancakes,' etc. This sentence can apply to absolutely anything within the context of Twelfth Night (though maybe not pancakes), so it's a good one just to have in your back pocket for any introduction.

PARAGRAPH 1 Shakespeare creates female characters which, in their independence and intellect, contravene the accepted gender norms[5] The most pertinent exemplar of this is "fair Olivia." In the wake of her father and brother's deaths Olivia is the 'lady of the house', whose wealth and influence is unmatched throughout Illyria except by Orsino, whose suit she rejects as "heresy." In this refusal to "marry above her station" she is sure to maintain the power that she has gained over her estate in any relationship. Furthermore, Olivia's "bestow of [Cesario]" with gifts, including "a ring" symbolic of marriage and the cyclical nature of love, are in contrast to the inactive tendency of women, described by Viola, to "pine... like Patience on as monument" rather than "t[ell] her love."[6] Olivia thus embodies a rejection of the patriarchy in her wilful reversal of the power dynamic between men and women implicit in this gender hierarchy. **PARAGRAPH 2** As well as demonstrating that females may be equal to males in status, the play demonstrates that women may be intellectually equal or even superior to men. This is evident in Maria's quick wittedness, which allows her to match wits with Feste – the "wise[st]" character and best "corrupter of words" in the play – and intellectually best Sir Andrew with a "dry jest." This is further substantiated by[7] the fact that it was entirely Maria's cunning that facilitated the creation and execution of the humiliating "gull[ing] into an ayword" of Malvolio.	5. Never assume that the person reading your work agrees with or even knows what you're talking about. If you use terms that may be ambiguous or subjective, like 'accepted gender norms', you must explain specifically what what you mean . For example, later in this paragraph I explain that 'accepted gender norms' refers to the inactive tendencies of women, and that Olivia's power is a reversal of the norm. for women during Shakespeare's time. 6. You may have been taught an acronym like 'TEAL' for your body paragraphs – Topic sentence, Evidence, Analysis, Link. But if you want to write better essays, keep the topic and linking sentences, but scratch the idea that 'evidence' and 'analysis' are two separate things, as combining both quotes and commentary in each sentence to make your approach more sophisticated. 7. This is like a sophisticated variation on terms like 'additionally' or 'furthermore.' Always use linking words and phrases that explain how your current point relates to the one before. This is important to make sure your paragraphs flow.

Although Orsino's mostly generalised statements about women being "fair flower[s that] once displayed... fall that very hour" exhibit the presence of gender stereotyping in Shakespeare's fictitious universe, the actions of the women in the play transcend this narrow definition; their "flower[s]" of independence, intelligence, and even beauty persist throughout the play. Furthermore, Orsino's own such statements are often contradictory,[8] varying within the same conversation in Act II Scene IV from calling men "more giddy and unfirm... than women" to asserting that "no woman... can bide the [strength of his] love" for Olivia. Thus, even Orsino's own view of gender roles reflects the variations between men and women as individuals, rather than as objects of their sex. However the feminist reader cannot only analyse the role of females within the text, as feminism by definition is about equality of gender, and thus *Twelfth Night's* portrayal of masculinity must also be considered.[9]

PARAGRAPH 3

The vast variety of male characters in *Twelfth Night* demonstrates a broad range of what may be considered masculine. In Malvolio, Shakespeare presents the man "of self-love", with "puritan[ical]" and "virtuous" tendencies. This narcissism and austerity finds its antithesis[10] in Sir Toby, a dishonest man who manipulates Sir Andrew for his money and concerns himself primarily with the pursuits of "quaffing and drinking." However, these two characters' differences in personality did not make either of them less valid as a specimen of masculinity, as both Malvolio and Sir Toby are validated in their manhood by the ability to judge it in others.

8. Just because a character says something, doesn't mean that something is true. Here, I point out Orsino's hypocrisies to show that his comments about women shouldn't be taken seriously. You always make your own argument stronger by addressing the other possible explanations, even when they contradict you, because if you leave them out entirely it looks like you forgot about them or are ignoring them, and either way your credibility will suffer.

9. This is another great sentence that I used in just about every essay (on any text!) that was relevant to a feminist critical lens. You can also take out the 'feminist' references and just make it a sentence about some other topic, like gender (e.g. 'However when considering gender, the reader cannot only analyse the role of females within the text; *Twelfth Night's* portrayal of masculinity must also be considered).

10. This is a great word to use when contrasting characters. Using sophisticated language can make your essays more impressive, but *be very careful!* Only use a word if you're sure you know what it means. I once read an essay where the student had put every third word into the thesaurus and replaced it with some five-syllable monstrosity. The trouble was, half of them really didn't mean what they thought they meant, or were totally wrong for the context. Making good points in plain English is a thousand times better than using fancy words that don't communicate your point!

Malvolio relays to Olivia "what manner of man" Cesario is, and Sir Toby often compares Sir Andrew to "any man in Illyria." Similarly, Sir Andrew and Sebastian provided opposing but equally supported models of manliness.[11] The former is a rich and learned knight, having "three thousand ducats a year" and "speak[ing] three or four languages," but "a coward" with "no more wit than... an ordinary man". Whilst Sebastian, conversely, is an ordinary man socio-economically speaking (like his sister, having lost everything in the shipwreck), but has the intelligence to reason logically when his "soul disputes well with [his] sense," and is skilled enough in fighting to give both Sir Andrew and Sir Toby "a bloody coxcomb." These far ranging personalities suggest masculinity to be a widely ranging concept rather than a fixed ideal.[12] Indeed, if any character is to represent the traditionally 'perfect man' it is Orsino, in the combination of his wealth and power as demonstrated by his numerous servants, and his education as demonstrated by his speaking in verse with wide ranging poetic images from "a bank of violets" to "the marble breasted tyrant." Therefore,[13] Olivia's rejection of the "suit from the count" represents the failure of traditional masculinity. The socially mandated pressure from men to define themselves as such by the courting of a woman and the attainment of power is also subverted in the play by Antonio's "desire, more sharp than filed steel" for Sebastian rather than for any woman, and by Feste's contentment for his "Foolery... [to shine] everywhere" rather than seeking a more powerful position with responsibility and stability. Thus, *Twelfth Night* portrays a spectrum within the terms 'male' and 'female.'[14] However it also presents a spectrum *between* them.	11. Again, pointing out various opposing examples makes an essay far more balanced and interesting than only focusing on examples that fall neatly into one category. 12. It can be tempting to separate something into what is called a 'false dichotomy' – oversimplifying a complex argument into two opposing sides – and then say that one answer is right and one is wrong. This analysis of masculinity is strong because instead of doing this, it recognises multiple different facets to the 'argument' (in this case, what masculinity is) and acknowledges that they can all be equally valid. 13. Always, always, finish making your point with a strong remark like this. Explain clearly and concisely what conclusion might be reached by the evidence you just gave or are bout to give, using linking words and phrases like 'Therefore,' 'Thus,' Hence,' etc. 14. This 'link' sentence ties together this paragraph to the ones above and the essay prompt. The next one 'links' down to the next paragraph, which helps to enhance essay cohesion.

PARAGRAPH 4

Shakespeare suggests through Twelfth Night the ambiguity of gender itself, showing how it may be fluid and non-binary. This is textually evident in the form of Viola; her abrupt and unprompted decision to "present [herself] as an eunuch", itself an identity considered neither woman nor quite man, suggests a deep rooted rejection of socially mandated gender binaries. Further, that her masculinity is never questioned, despite feminine qualities such as has her "smooth and rubious... lip," evidence that gender is performative rather than implicit. This concept takes on added significance when it is considered that the original actors of the play were all male, and thus some of them 'performed' as female throughout their career.[15] However, these explorations of the ambiguity of gender and gender roles ultimately serve as reinforcement of the stricter, more 'traditional' binary definitions of gender and patriarchal prejudices that facilitate the oppression of women.[16] Firstly, it must be noted that the ratio of male to female characters in *Twelfth Night* is grossly unequal; there are twelve male characters as opposed to only three females, one of whom spends the majority of the play presenting as a boy. While it may be argued that[17] Viola's disguise empowers her, the fact that such an act is necessary shows that men are advantaged over women in the world of Illyria. Furthermore, Viola herself acknowledges that such a "disguise [is] a wickedness", in that it ultimately causes the "thriftless sighs" of heartache in a fellow woman.

15. Remember that *Twelfth Night* is first and foremost a play! Unlike a novel, it's meant to be performed live, and reference to this fact can give extra dimension to your discussion that just isn't available with other texts.
16. What?! Flipping your argument in the middle of the essay? That can't be right! Actually, developing your argument throughout the essay, so long as it is logical and doesn't contradict earlier observations, is excellent!
17. This is a useful phrase for acknowledging and responding to other interpretations.

Although the demonstrated social benefits of maleness over womanhood maybe explained as realism rather than sexism, the correlation of treatment of characters during play's denouement according to whether and how they departed from gender norms in action and characterisation during the plot's period of 'misrule' cannot.

PARAGRAPH 5

Although Olivia is a woman of wealth and independence, in this she is an outlier (whereas there are multiple male knights and captains), and she ends to play trapped in "a contract of eternal bond" not with the 'Cesario' that she fell in love with, but Sebastian; a man she does not know who (in accordance with Elizabethan marital laws) will rule her life. Likewise, Antonio and Sir Andrew and do not comply with traditional masculinity, in giving the "sanctity of love" to a man rather than a woman and being an "idiot[ic]" "coward," respectively,[18] and accordingly neither end play with love. The individuals that are 'rewarded' in the final act are Orsino, who throughout the play exemplified the traditionally romanticised masculine archetype of the "give[r of] unsought" and unrequited love, and Viola, whose blind devotion to the former makes her willing to die "a thousand deaths," as they end up with each other. This pairing off of characters into marriages perpetuates the oppression of the female party (as she becomes a piece of her "master's" property) and, in its binary nature, leaves no room for gender ambiguity. This is consistent with the concept of 'Twelfth Night,' literally the twelfth night of the Festival of Saturnalia.

18. When you list two things and then describe those things in the same order you can explain what you have done by saying 'respectively' (e.g. 'Sophie and Max's favourite colours are blue and green, respectively' means that Sophie's favourite colour is blue and Max's is green).

Just as historically this was a time of licensed misrule that served to placate the slave and serving classes for the remainder of the year, the explorations of gender fluidity and female empowerment in Shakespeare's play are a form of permitted 'incorrectness' designed to strengthen the eventual return to strict gender roles and thereby female subjugation.[19] These restrictive aspects subtly pervade play, even during the period of 'misrule', in the preoccupation with females having "radient... beauty" and males proving their "valour." **CONCLUSION** In his play *Twelfth Night,* William Shakespeare[20] presents characters and situations that suggest the ambiguity of gender roles, but ultimately reaffirms rigid and repressive prejudices regarding gender. A feminist reading of the text may therefore find Shakespeare's treatment of men and women therein to be traditionalist and damaging by modern standards.[21] However, the deviation from stereotypical gender norms, irrespective of the play's final abolishment of such deviations, does indicate that such norms are socially constructed and may therefore be transcended.	19. This is another great sentence that can be applied to almost anything in *Twelfth Night.* It shows that you've done your research and have a broader, more contextual view of analysis than just the text itself. 20. Conventionally, conclusions should once again state the title of the text and the full name of the author, as a signal that you're making your closing remarks. 21. Shakespeare's plays are old! Acknowledging your own modern biases shows a self-awareness that lends credibility to your argument.

Essay Three

QUESTION: How does Shakespeare craft meaning in his play *Twelfth Night?*

ESSAY	COMMENTS
INTRODUCTION In his play *Twelfth Night,* William Shakespeare manipulates both specific textual elements including dialogue and sequencing, as well as more intangible factors such as tone, in order to present his own unique perspective on the play's themes of love and madness.[1] **PARAGRAPH 1** The fundamental requirements of Shakespeare's medium of theatre, as opposed to films or novels, necessitates the use of different techniques to impart deeper meaning to the audience. Shakespeare's personal style as a playwright shuns stage directions except where unavoidable, and thus subtextual understanding must be derived from imagery and metaphor explicit in his characters' dialogue.[2] Such reliance on the use of language to drive scenic atmosphere, whether of wistful "barful strife" or of jubilant "fooling", and explore theme is evident even from Orsino's opening declaration to the "spirit of love". The imagery and themes established therein of "music... love... [and] the sea" set the tone of melancholic reflection that has a cohesion throughout the play; music makes its return in the lyrics of Feste's despondent reflections on the implications of of "youth" inevitably giving way to "death" for "true love," and the image of the ocean continually manifests itself both literally and in the protagonists' "salt water" tears.	1. This introduction is short and specific, listing some of the things that will be touched on in the essay. Writing an introduction like this can be difficult if you're unsure of where exactly you're going with your essay, but it can also serve as a concise foundation for later exploration. 2. Analysis of the metalanguage and construction of the play shows off your understanding of literary terminology and technique, while also demonstrating an ability to step back from the nitty-gritty plot details and consider the bigger picture.

Onstage, it is far easier for these images to be established though spoken allusions to "salt waves" than to have actual water or wave-like stagecraft. Although such spoken imagery may evoke a less visceral response from the audience than a physical manifestation of said image, Shakespeare's use of poetry utilises the musicality of cadence and rhyme to bypass the literal and logical thought processes applied to spoken language, thus unlocking the audience's more abstract consideration of the concepts and images presented.[3] For example, the poetic evocation of Orsino's love being "all hungry as the sea" in Act 2 Scene 4, in which Orsino and Viola (as Cesario) emotionally compare the strength of "passion" between a man and "woman's heart," exemplifies Shakespeare's use of the crashing ocean as pathetic fallacy[4] and allows him to thereby impose the sea's significance as a metaphor for the depths of human emotion. However, in his emphasis on written text with little physically actionable instruction, Shakespeare's play creates ambiguity surrounding gestures and movements which could significantly impact the audience's understanding of the play. For example, although there is potential for sexually charged moments between Olivia and Cesario and between Orsino and Viola, textually supported in the witty reportage between them but not explicitly included, Shakespeare's decline to write stage directions mean that it could with equal validity be performed with no chemistry at all. With such adaptions, any director of this work could drastically alter the meaning of the play even while remaining faithful to the text. It must therefore be asked what the messages of the original are.

3. This is a long sentence that basically means 'Shakespeare can't literally make us see and feel stuff with words, but because he uses poetry he can get pretty close.'

4. Note the consistent use of metalanguage and structural features throughout this paragraph. This helps to showcase your understanding of the text's composition to your marker.

PARAGRAPH 2 The chronology of Shakespeare's script manipulates the audience's understanding in ways mere characterisation cannot. As Olivia is reminded when "the clock upbraids [her] with [its] waste," time an important and limited resource with massive significance. Accordingly, Shakespeare's deliberate configuration of scene sequence, or 'timeline,' is very noteworthy. His choices of first and second scene mean that Orsino's passionate poeticism in admiration of "music [as] the food of love" occurs *before* the introduction of the protagonist Viola, and her subsequent wish that she "[her]self would be [Orsino's] wife" occurs in her very first scene with him. This minimises Viola's time spent with Orsino and deprives the audience of a chance to witness their mutual falling into love. Consequently their relationship appears implausible, especially to a modern audience,[5] and demonstrates Viola's naivety and Orsino's "very opal mind." This characterisation of Orsino, opal being a stone renowned for the fickle changeability of its colours under the light, make his proposition to make Viola his "mistress" in the play's denouement seem more an act of opportunism than love. Shakespeare also includes other illogical character reactions, such as Viola's lack of response upon hearing Antonio call her "Sebastian," which serve to make Viola and the rest of the character's actions appear as irrational as possible. Perhaps[6] Shakespeare's original intent in this, his characters' "even so quick... catch[ing of]" love, was the exaggeration of the text's "improbable fiction" – a meta-theatrical nod to the play's primary purpose as a comedy designed, as Feste notes, "to please" the masses "every day."	5. This sentence explains the consequence of the character's actions with regards to its effect on the audience, which (when done well) is far more sophisticated than explaining the consequence of characters' actions on other characters. 6. Always acknowledge the opposite potential interpretation. It makes it look like you've thought of everything, so increases your credibility.

However, this analysis is inconsistent with Shakespeare's presentation of even stock comic characters such as Sir Andrew as complex and multifaceted in quieter moments that elicit audience empathy, such as Sir Andrew's having been "adored once." Beyond character and plot, the author's scattered construction of the play also cannot be explained away by the play's status as a 'comedy', such as the drastic juxtaposition of tone and setting between the love-lorn melancholy in Orsino's castle in Act 2 Scene 4 and the riotous pranking of Malvolio in Olivia's garden at the very next scene. Rather, a better explanation may be offered in considering the tone elicited by the play as a whole; *Twelfth Night's* chronology reflects the atmosphere of the play, which may be said to operate in the realms of "midsummer madness." **PARAGRAPH 3** The structure of *Twelfth Night* elicits a particular tone and thereby a particular meaning, reflective of the theme presented as most significant: madness.[7] Shakespeare ends the play with Malvolio's declaration to be "revenged", his "notorious... abuse" in juxtaposition against the coupling of the play's protagonists and so leaving the audience with a sour critique of society, Shakespeare's warning that the common man's "fun" at the expense of "puritan[s]" such as Malvolio could not endure (interestingly, this prediction is historically upheld). This makes contentious the play's categorisation as a 'comedy,' as it does not meet the definition that all plot aspects in such a play are resolved.	7. If you're unsure of exactly how to word a sentence like this, you can leave a gap here and come back afterwards to fill in the gap with a key word or phrase like 'madness' later. It's fine to start vague with an introduction or topic sentence as this allows to you explore your thoughts throughout your paragraph as they arrive. Just remember to read back through and make sure it still makes sense when you're done.

Indeed, although Shakespeare includes many indisputably funny scenes and situations, such as the reveal of Malvolio in his "yellow stockings" and the fight between Cesario and Sir Andrew, much of the play muses on darker topics, such as Feste's contemplation of his "part of death" and the futility of love. Indeed, love itself is depicted by Shakespeare as an irrational form of madness, whereby every character which succumbs to "passion" finds themselves in a worse position than they began with. For example, Antonio's "love" for Sebastian finds him arrested and without his purse, Olivia describes her love for Cesario as "merry madness" and because of the rash and foolish state of mind it puts her into marries a stranger, and Malvolio's pursuit of Olivia sees him "locked" in "darkness." Even the aforementioned scenes designed to evoke laughter, when analysed more objectively, place a lens on the extent of human cruelty to one another, as Maria and Sir Toby's manipulations of others "in the name of jesting" is always to the victim's detriment. This, in addition to the previously discussed structural aspects, place a particular focus on different forms of "madness" and makes the audience uncomfortably aware of the negative aspects of the play. This meditative perspective is affirmed and accentuated by Feste's final song's lyrics; The song outlines the difficulties faced when one grows from "a little tiny boy... to [a] man", as "men shut their gate[s]" against one another and "could... never thrive," difficulties manifested in the uncontrollable "wind and the rain." Shakespeare ends the play with Feste's metatheatrical acknowledgement of the "play [being] done," thus inviting the audience to consciously consider what they have watched in all its melancholy.[8]	8. This is an analytical acknowledgement of making an analysis while pointing out a character's acknowledgement of being in a play is about as next-level meta as you can get! Overall though, this is an effective paragraph conclusion that ties together lots of the different threads that have been discussed here.

CONCLUSION William Shakespeare presents, in his play *Twelfth Night,* a meditation on madness and the transience of life, in the guise of a romantic comedy. However, this is not to imply that a more sanguine interpretation, or indeed any other that may be derived from the text, is incorrect or less valid than this analysis.[9] As the alternative title of 'Twelfth Night' suggests, the play and its messages may be taken as 'What You' – what any reader – 'Will'.	9. Mentioning possible alternate interpretations can add another dimension to your essay, as this is a testament to your broader understanding of the nature of the text and its multilayered meaning.

Essay Four

QUESTION: How does Shakespeare depict privilege in his play *Twelfth Night?*

ESSAY	COMMENTS
INTRODUCTION In *Twelfth Night,* William Shakespeare presents characters from all across the spectrum[1] of privilege, within a crafted world whose hierarchical structures are reminiscent of our own. The contrastingly fantastical events therein thus provide a crucible through which the Bard challenges not only his fictional depiction of men and women, the rich and poor, powerful and powerless,[2] but also those of society in such a manner as to exploit the perceived rigidity of these dichotomies[3] for comic effect. **PARAGRAPH 1** In Maria, Shakespeare presents an embodiment of the oppressed. She is the only character who is both a female and a member of the proletariat. Although Viola dresses and acts as a "servant", she is simultaneously treated with the respect evoked by her male "disguise" that sees her entrusted with "some four or five attend[ants]", and is in truth has "right noble... blood" and comes from a family with "bounteous" "gold". Maria, by contrast, is a "gentlewoman" to Olivia and thus possesses one of the lowest positional statuses of the play. Therefore, in her well-rounded character and positively connotative traits, Shakespeare passes comment on the redundancy of patriarchal and capitalist societies.	1. Calling it a 'spectrum' ensures that we don't fall into the pitfall of creating a false dichotomy. 2. Here, a group of three (or tricolon) is used, which helps the flow of the sentence and gives us three different sub-topics to explore once we get into the evidence in the body paragraphs. 3. Acknowledge that others might see what we have identified as a spectrum to be binary, without judgement, to show that you've considered it but reached a more developed conclusion.

Maria proves her wit and sexual empowerment in her very first scene when she invites Sir Andrew to touch "th'buttery-bar" – evident by the lewd context of the latter's attempted "accost" to refer to Maria's breast – in "a dry jest," being a figurative caustic joke and a literal demonstration of her lack of attraction to him.[4] Such physical self awareness and self-confidence is also displayed by other women in the play, as in Olivia's understanding of her own "well done" "beauty" and un-submissive refusal of "Orsino's suit." Although Viola dresses as a man and thus hides rather than embraces her feminine sexuality, she does thereby evidence her equally un-submissive nature in defying the sumptuary laws of the Renaissance.By contrast, the majority of the male characters use womens' appearances to justify their objectification, seeking to dominate Olivia due to her "sweet perfections" at the expense of "all affections else", "to crush [her spirit] a little [so] it would bend to me." Similar to her qualities being representative of all women characters, Maria's employment of double meanings and "excellent...wit" is also demonstrated by the other key representatives of the proletariat; Feste's "dally[ance] with words" and Sir Toby's "admirable fooling". Their use of prose contrasts the bourgeoisie's "poetical" evidence of learning, yet these three lower class individuals' clever manipulation of Malvolio demonstrates a greater level of cognitive capacity than their rich masters; Orsino and Olivia fail to see through Viola's disguise despite close observance of her "all [being] semblative of a woman's part" and her own confessions of being "not that I play." Thus, Shakespeare mocks the privileged classes. His evocation of individuals, however, is far more nuanced.	4. This displays an strong understanding of how meaning can be layered, as closely examining this quote reveals a range of different ideas we can unpack to build up this interpretation.

PARAGRAPH 2

Sir Toby could – as a knight and relative to the rich Olivia – be considered bourgeois. However it is evident that he undercuts this title by wasting all his personal wealth on "revelry," such that he is poor enough to need to filch off of Sir Andrew's "three-thousand ducats a year", and dishonoured enough to be reprimanded by a mere "steward."[5] This lack of respect for the authority of the upper echelons is mirrored by Sir Toby's contrasting respect for Maria. He treats Maria as an equal in intelligence by his entreaty of her to "possess us, tell us" her plan for revenge on Malvolio rather than continuing with his own. In addition, unlike Olivia's suitors, he offers to "become [Maria's] bondslave" rather than master. Sir Toby thus rejects the social hierarchy in a manner that could be considered both Marxist and feminist.[6] Furthermore, as he is a comic character Shakespeare encourages his audience to like and identify with Sir Toby, thus it could be construed that this character's anti-authoritarian ideals were designed to be didactic. However, this is not to say that *Twelfth Night* presents an egalitarian fantasy. In fact, quite the opposite is true.

PARAGRAPH 3

Despite the defiance and rejection of stereotypes befitting a capitalist patriarchy by intelligent and highly capable women and worker characters in *Twelfth Night*, Shakespeare's Illyria and play as a whole still favour the rich and the masculine. Indeed, such favour is built into the play's very structure.

5. Acknowledging the limitations of labels, once again, shows that you're engaging with the texts critically and creatively.

6. Here's the other cool thing about critical perspectives; you can use more than one! As a matter of fact, often different critical lenses will correlate and give more depth to each other. For example, if 'nature' is personified (and it usually is) as a 'she' in a text, both eco-criticism and feminism may apply.

Viola, as the character who facilitates the most confusion in the play and around whose disguise the plot begins and ends, would ostensibly be the play's protagonist.[7] However the entire first scene is given not to Viola, but to "Count" Orsino (the antithesis to Maria as a rich male), thus displaying the epitome of bourgeois male privilege. Similarly, Orsino gives numerous long speeches about "the passion of [his] love", as indeed Malvolio spends and entire scene fantasising bout being "Count Malvolio!... married to" Olivia, whereas the women's dialogue serves primarily to further the plot or briefly summarise it. For example, Viola's first soliloquy muses less on her thoughts and more on explaining to the audience that "[Olivia] loves me [Viola]... [Orsino] loves her dearly, / And I [Viola] fond as much on him." It must also be noted that there are only three female characters in the play, such that irrespective of how well-depicted they may be they cannot possibly represent all facets of femininity as fully as the multitude of male characters do masculinity.[8]

PARAGRAPH 4

Whatever independence the women and proletariat are permitted during the chaotic midsection of the play is taken away at the end.[9] Olivia's fate is particularly punitive, being tricked into losing her wealth and independence (in accordance with Elizabethan marriage laws) to a stranger rather than the "Cesario" that she fell in "love" with. This is reflective of the threat that she posed not only to the patriarchy as "the lady of" her own "house", but to the class system by refusing to "marry above her station."

7. It's good to balance analyses of specific scenes and actions with a more broad view of structure and metalanguage, to make sure that you're examining the text from every possible angle.
8. There's that wonderful sentence again. Seriously, if you plan on talking about gender even a little bit, make this sentence your own!
9. Though not compulsory, structuring your essay to loosely follow the trajectory of the plot so that your final paragraph is talking about the play's end can be particularly impressive.

Similarly, for seeking to rise above his servile station in life and become "Count Malvolio!" her steward finds himself "notoriously abused." Even Sir Toby, rejector of hierarchy, enjoys the benefits of male privilege in thoughtlessly commanding Maria to fetch "a stoup of wine," and of his position in putting down Malvolio for being a mere "steward," demonstrating the deeply ingrained sexism and elitism of the society. Thus, somewhat ironically, Shakespeare frames the "improbable fiction" of the play's events in a world that reflected all too realistically that of his time, and, a feminist or Marxist critic might conclude, of our own today society.[10] **CONCLUSION** The only character which seems to exist outside of these structures in his ability to "walk... the orb like the sun" without consequence is Feste,[11] whose meta-textual observance of "our play" supports this air of omniscient objectivity. Therefore it is telling that Shakespeare's final comment in *Twelfth Night*, despite all of the marriages that many might interpret as an archetypal 'happily ever after', is a contrastingly negative pathetic fallacy; in a world of irrepressible inequality, "the rain it raineth every day."	10. Furthermore, it's often good to make remarks that explicitly reference either Shakespeare's Elizabethan audience, or our own contemporary context, as this shows the assessor that you understand the impact texts can have across time. 11. This might seem like an unconventional start to a conclusion, and it is! Normally we'd open by naming the play or the author, and making a general comment about the message of the play... but some rules are made to be broken! There are only a few conventions you must abide (such as ensuring your essay has a logical flow of ideas) – everything else depends on your personal preference, style, and essay topic.